QUILT BLOCKS
for Beginners

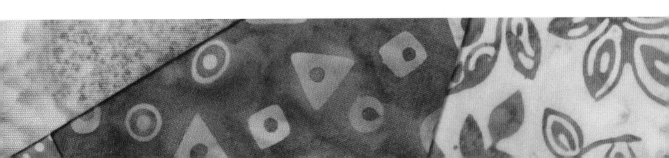

Quarto.com

© 2025 Quarto Publishing Group USA Inc.
Text © 2013 Quarto Publishing Group USA Inc.

First Published in 2025 by New Shoe Press, an imprint of The Quarto Group,
100 Cummings Center, Suite 265-D, Beverly, MA 01915, USA.
T (978) 282-9590 F (978) 283-2742

Essential, In-Demand Topics, Four-Color Design, Affordable Price
New Shoe Press publishes affordable, beautifully designed books covering evergreen, in-demand subjects. With a goal to inform and inspire readers' everyday hobbies, from cooking and gardening to wellness and health to art and crafts, New Shoe titles offer the ultimate library of purposeful, how-to guidance aimed at meeting the unique needs of each reader. Reimagined and redesigned from Quarto's best-selling backlist, New Shoe books provide practical knowledge and opportunities for all DIY enthusiasts to enrich and enjoy their lives.

Visit Quarto.com/New-Shoe-Press for a complete listing of the New Shoe Press books.

New Shoe Press titles are also available at discount for retail, wholesale, promotional, and bulk purchase. For details, contact the Special Sales Manager by email at specialsales@quarto.com or by mail at The Quarto Group, Attn: Special Sales Manager, 100 Cummings Center, Suite 265-D, Beverly, MA 01915, USA.

10 9 8 7 6 5 4 3 2 1

ISBN: 978-0-7603-9088-7
eISBN: 978-0-7603-9089-4

The content in this book was previously published in *The Quilt Block Book* (Creative Publishing international 2013) by Nancy Wick.

Library of Congress Cataloging-in-Publication Data available

Illustrations: Nancy Wick
Photographs: Glenn Scott Photography

Printed in China

QUILT BLOCKS
for Beginners

Fresh, Versatile Designs for Quilts, Clothes, Accessories, and Decor

NANCY WICK

NEW SHOE PRESS

Contents

Introduction

I started quilting after my grandmother died as a way of feeling closer to her. She had been a quilter, and would be amazed by all the tools and gadgets I use in my craft. She cut and sewed "the old-fashioned" way, without using a sewing machine or rotary cutter. My first quilt-related memory is of a Double-Wedding Ring quilt my grandmother had made. I thought it was so beautiful. As a small child, I remember aching for the day when I was grown up and could have a Double-Wedding Ring quilt of my own, as I thought only married women could have one. To learn the art of quilt making, I purchased my first quilt book, took a class at a local quilt shop, and forevermore I have been passionate about making quilts. Like my grandmother, I am a product of the times in which I grew up. She learned to sew and cut her pieces by hand, whereas I learned to sew on a machine. Now I enjoy using my computerized sewing machine in creative and innovative ways.

One of the things I like most about the quilt-making process is that it is never boring. There is always a new block to learn or a new technique to try. With this book, I encourage new and experienced quilters to experiment with three quilt-making techniques: traditional-pieced blocks, foundation-pieced blocks, and appliqué blocks. Each section begins with an overview of the basic techniques and tools used for that method of sewing quilt blocks. The block patterns in each section—each designed with a fresh, modern twist—include patterns and/or cutting instructions. These quilt blocks represent a fraction of the possible quilt blocks, but provide a solid foundation for quilters of all skill levels. Study the sewn blocks and quilt layout illustrations to help you select your fabrics. For even greater creative potential, try varying the color placement, value, and texture of the fabric for the blocks. Invert the dark and light fabrics in a block, for example, and you may discover a striking new color combination; when you combine those blocks, a secondary pattern may emerge. Let these blocks serve as inspiration any time you are in the mood to sew a quilt.

If you are new to quilting, a traditional-pieced block is a good place to start. Most of the quilt blocks in this section are provided in three different sizes, so feel free to mix and match the blocks, creating endless design possibilities. Foundation-pieced blocks offer precision and accuracy, especially with small and sharply angled pieces. With this method, patches of fabric are sewn to a foundation paper marked with the block pattern, eliminating the concern for sewing accurate ¼" (6 mm) seams. Many quilters find the precision of foundation piecing exciting and versatile once they master the technique because they can tackle a block they would never dream of piecing in a traditional way. Appliqué blocks offer a wonderful opportunity to explore the stitches on your sewing machine, and can really help add another layer of visual interest to a quilt. Appliqué block patterns are appealing because the technique is far more forgiving than piecing. Unlike piecing, if fabrics shift slightly, it makes little difference to the final product.

Each of the blocks includes a sample quilt layout to help you envision how a quilt made with that particular block might look. Use the sample quilt layout as a source of inspiration; it is by no means the only way to set that block into a quilt. Feel free to mix and match all of the provided blocks and make your mark on the design by combining the blocks in unique ways. After making enough blocks for a quilt, audition different arrangements before sewing them into a finished quilt top. Different patterns will emerge as you rotate blocks; try setting them horizontally, on-point, or off-set. Sometimes as you rotate the blocks, a secondary pattern presents itself, and that is always a delightful surprise. Select the arrangement you find most pleasing, and sew the blocks into a quilt top.

My hope is that you use this book to learn a new pattern or technique, and I wish you many hours of sewing joy. Further, I hope my enthusiasm for quilt making is infectious. Quilting has brought me much enjoyment, and I should not be the only one having this much fun! I cherish that quilt making is my legacy, and by making and giving quilts to my family and friends, I am indelibly stitching my love of quilts into the lives of those I care about. Just as my grandmother's quilts have left an impression on me, the stitches I've made in each of my quilts will remain long after I am gone.

—Nancy Wick

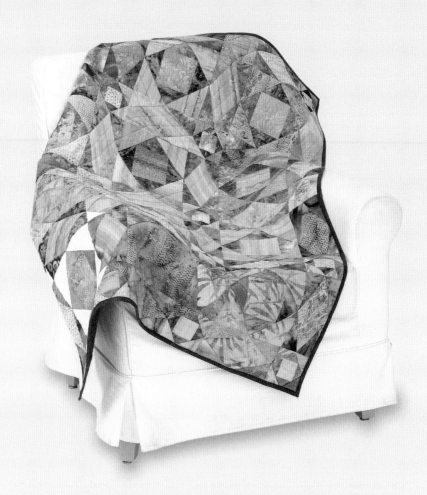

Traditional-Pieced Blocks

There is something serendipitous about taking big pieces of fabric, cutting them up into little pieces, and sewing the pieces back together into a big piece of fabric again. The process is full of unexpected, delightful surprises. In the pieced-block method, geometric shapes—squares, triangles, rectangles, and circles—are cut and sewn into blocks, which can be arranged into a quilt top or other project. This may be the most common method for making quilt blocks, as there are thousands of recognized pieced-block designs, and the possibilities are seemingly endless.

Tools and Supplies

Sewing machine: Any straight-stitch sewing machine in good working order is suitable for piecing. The following sewing machine features are desirable, but not necessary: needle down, free-hand knee lift, automatic thread cutter, adjustable needle positions, front-loading bobbin, adjustable stitch length/width, and adjustable presser foot pressure.

Straight stitch plate: Many sewing machines offer a straight stitch throat plate as an optional accessory. A straight stitch plate improves piecing accuracy, especially at the beginning and ends of seams since the needle hole of the plate is much smaller. It prevents fabric distortion and provides more control. Unlike a straight stitch plate, the wider hole of the zigzag throat plate allows the fabric to flex more around the needle, and it can push the fabric into the hole, causing gathers and puckers.

¼-inch presser foot: A quarter-inch (6 mm) foot helps ensure an accurate seam allowance. If one is not available for your machine, consider purchasing a generic one, such as Little Foot. Depending on your model of sewing machine, you may need to purchase a shank adapter to use the Little Foot on your sewing machine.

Seam guide: Some sewing machines offer an adjustable seam guide to screw into the bed of the sewing machine that makes guiding the fabric to the needle while maintaining an accurate ¼-inch (6 mm) seam allowance easier. If one is not available for your machine, consider marking the bed of the machine with masking tape, taking care not to cover the feed dogs.

Thread: The type of thread used in quilt block construction is important to the accuracy of the finished block. If you sew with a perfect ¼-inch (6 mm) seam, but use too thick thread, the finished block is too small since there is no allowance for the weight of the thread and the bend of the fabric as the seam is pressed. For best results, use a 50/3 or 60/3 cotton thread. Either match the piecing thread to the fabric, or consider using a neutral color such as a medium gray. Do not use a thread that contrasts sharply in color from the fabric, as it may be visible after pressing the quilt block.

Pins: Super-thin silk pins are best for piecing quilt blocks. They glide into the fabric easily and are less bulky than traditional pins. Normal pins can distort the fabric and be more inaccurate, which defeats the purpose of pinning in the first place. Generally, pins labeled as quilting pins are too thick and prevent the seam from lying flat while sewing.

(continued)

Sewing machine needles: For 50/3 thread, use a 75/11 Topstitch, Quilting, or Sharp needle. For 60/3 thread, use a 70/10 or 75/11 Topstitch, Quilting, or Sharp needle. Sharps have a very thin point and create perfectly straight stitches for accurate piecing. On the other hand, Quilting needles have a special tapered design to improve fabric penetration. Topstitch needles achieve perfectly straight stitches and have an extra-long eye.

Seam ripper: Look for one with a very fine sharp point and a comfortable handle.

Rotary cutter: A 45 mm or 60 mm rotary cutter is the best choice for cutting pieces for quilt construction. These sizes of rotary cutter are capable of cutting through up to eight layers of fabric at a time. In addition, there are cutters with ergonomic handles, which can make cutting for extended periods more comfortable.

Rotary mat: A 24" × 36" (61 × 91.4 cm) mat is versatile for all cuts. Rotary mats are self-healing and extend the life of the rotary cutter blade.

Rotary ruler: Start with a 6" × 24" (15.25 × 61 cm) and 12" × 12" (30.5 × 30.5 cm) ruler that includes 45- and 60-degree markings. Use a 6" × 24" (15.25 × 61 cm) ruler to make initial cuts from yardage, and use a 12" × 12" (30.5 × 30.5 cm) ruler for squaring blocks. Having a 6" × 6" (15.25 × 15.25 cm) and 6" × 12" (15.25 × 30.5 cm) ruler will make secondary cuts easier.

Iron and ironing board: Use an iron that is in good working order, with a cotton temperature setting. Many quilters prefer an iron without an auto-off feature.

Temporary double-stick tape: Useful for adhering a paper template to the fabric to prevent the template from shifting while rotary cutting.

Thread snips: Spring loaded, always in the open position, are a good choice.

Scissors: Serrated edge with 4" (10 cm) and 8" (20 cm) blades.

Stiletto: Some people find a stiletto handy for guiding the fabric under the presser foot. You can also use a bamboo skewer or an orange stick.

Tweezers: Bent tip tweezers are helpful for feeding the fabric under the presser foot, especially when doing curved piecing.

Freezer paper: Freezer paper—from the grocery store—comes in a roll, and is useful for cutting templates and blocking quilt squares. When ironed to fabric, the waxy side sticks temporarily to allow for accurate cutting without pinning.

Fabric Preparation

Take the time to pre-wash fabric to reduce the risk of colors bleeding when the quilt is laundered. Some fabric colors (such as red, blue, and purple) bleed easily, transferring excess dye from the manufacturing process to lighter colored fabrics in the quilt. To test a fabric for color fastness, place a small sample in a bowl of warm, sudsy water for a few seconds. Stir the fabric around the bowl for a bit and place it on a white, terry-cloth towel. If there is any dye transfer to the towel, that fabric is not colorfast. With these fabrics, consider adding a product such as Synthrapol to the wash cycle of the washing machine to help set the dye. (Synthrapol is available online or at many quilt shops). The final step in fabric preparation is to press and starch the fabric, which increases accuracy during the cutting and piecing process.

Rotary Cutting

A rotary cutter looks like a pizza wheel and has revolutionized quilt making. It uses a super-sharp blade to roll through multiple layers of fabric. By guiding the blade along the edge of a rotary ruler, accurate and speedy cuts are possible. Replace the blade when the rotary cutter skips or no longer cuts easily. Cut strips of fabric from the crosswise grain (perpendicular to the selvages). Make a secondary cut from these strips to create geometric shapes (such as squares, triangles, and rectangles) for creating the pieced block. Taking time to cut precisely will pay off in the end, as pieces will fit together well, and seams will match.

Strip Cutting

1. To cut strips from a 45" (114 cm) piece of fabric, fold the fabric selvages together and align the edges so the fabric fold lies smooth and does not pucker. If the fold does not lie flat, adjust one selvage edge to either the right or left until it does.

2. Make a clean-up cut along the entire length of the right edge of the fabric. First, lay the fabric on the rotary cutting mat with the folded edge closest to your body. Then place a 6" × 24" (15.25 × 61 cm) ruler along the right edge of the fabric, with the bulk of the fabric to your left. Align one of the horizontal lines on the ruler with the bottom edge of the folded fabric.

3. Place the rotary cutting blade against the ruler's edge and roll it across the fabric, making a clean, straight cut. Prevent the ruler from shifting during long cuts by stopping periodically and moving your hand up the ruler so that it is even with the cutter.

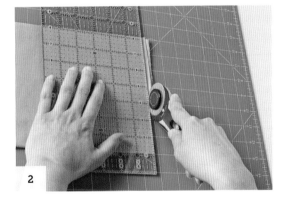

(continued)

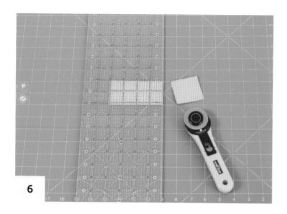

6

Cutting from Templates

Some quilt blocks require the use of templates. Use a template when a block requires curved piecing, or when the units in the block include an angle not easily measured with a rotary cutting ruler. The templates provided include the seam allowance. The solid line represents the finished unit, and the dashed line represents the cutting line.

4. Rotate the cutting mat 180 degrees so that the folded edge of the fabric is now on the top. To make a measured cut, align the appropriate vertical line on the ruler with the cut edge of the fabric, and align a horizontal line on the ruler with the fold of the fabric.

5. Place the rotary cutting blade against the ruler and cut the fabric along the edge, making a clean, straight cut. Prevent the ruler from shifting during long cuts by stopping periodically and moving your hand up the ruler so that it is even with the cutter.

6. Once a strip of fabric is cut, rotate the strip 45 degrees and sub-cut it into the required sub-units (such as square or rectangles) using the same cutting techniques used for cutting strips. Cut triangles from either squares or rectangles, dissecting the unit diagonally.

1. Copy the template onto plastic template material or regular paper. Roughly, cut out the shape, approximately ⅛" (3 mm) past the dotted line. Do not cut on the dotted line at this time.

2. To prevent the template from shifting while cutting, adhere the template to the right side of the fabric with a piece of double-sided, temporary tape.

3. Using a rotary cutter, cut precisely on the dotted line. For straight template lines, use a ruler with the rotary cutter. For curved template lines, use a rotary cutter and slowly cut on the dotted line.

If using freezer paper as a template, pre-shrink the paper by dry-pressing it, waxy side down, to the ironing board. Then peel it from the ironing surface, trace the template, and re-iron it onto the fabric.

Sewing

If your seam is too big or too small, fitting the sub-units together in the block is challenging. An inaccurate seam allowance usually translates to one (or both) of these scenarios: easing in fullness and puckered seams, or mismatched points. Neither of these make for an enjoyable sewing experience, so taking a few moments to set up your machine for an accurate ¼" (6 mm) seam allowance will reward you in the end.

By investing a few minutes at the beginning of the project to make a practice block, you can save yourself frustration later in the project.

CHECKING FOR AN ACCURATE SEAM ALLOWANCE:

- Place a piece of ¼" (6 mm) graph paper under the presser foot of your machine.

- Place the needle down so that it enters the graph paper at the intersection of a vertical and horizontal line.

- Lower the presser foot. A ¼" (6 mm) presser foot should line up with the next ¼" line on the graph paper.

If the presser foot does not line up with the next ¼" (6 mm) line on the graph paper, and your machine has adjustable needle positions, you can either move the needle position so that it does align, or you can add a seam guide to your machine.

To test the accuracy of your seam, cut three 1½" × 4" (3.8 × 10.2 cm) pieces of fabric. Sew the three strips together along the long edges. The width of the finished unit should measure 3½" (8.9 cm) exactly. If it is more than 3½" (8.9 cm), your seam is too small.

On the other hand, if it is less than 3½" (8.9 cm), your seam is too large. Also, measure the width of the center strip on the right side of the fabric. If the seam allowance is accurate, this strip should measure 1" (2.5 cm).

Finally, when testing the seam allowance, factor in the stitching line and pressing fold. Rotary cutters and rulers cut fabrics precisely, but when a seam is sewn and pressed open, the unit may be smaller than intended. For this reason, quilters strive for a scant (1 or 2 threads less than) ¼" (6 mm) seam to allow for the width of the stitching line and the fold of the fabric when it is pressed. Surprisingly, the width of the stitches and the fold of the fabric can really add up over the number of seams in a quilt. To demonstrate, if there are eight seams in a quilt block, this could amount to $\frac{8}{32}$" (6 mm). Multiply this by the number of blocks in a quilt, and you can see how this adds up quickly.

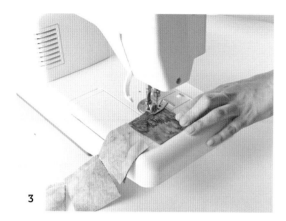

3

To Sew Pieced Blocks

1. With right sides together, place fabric A against fabric B, taking care to perfectly align the raw edges.

2. Sew a straight, ¼" (6 mm) seam. If sewing with a ¼" (6 mm) presser foot, align the fabric directly beneath the foot. The fabric edge should not be visible on the right side of the foot.

3. If making several units that are the same, "chain piece" them. After sewing one unit, feed the next unit under the presser foot without cutting the thread. After sewing, there will be a small piece of thread connecting units together. Snip this thread to separate the units.

4. Press seam allowances in the direction advised in the block instructions.

5. Sew sub-units into blocks, pressing with the addition of each sub-unit. Continue in this manner until the block is constructed.

Sometimes, it is necessary to pin this intersection together before sewing so the fabric does not shift. To do this, place the fabrics with right sides together. Place a pin through the wrong side of one fabric and the right side of the other fabric, exactly at the intersection point, pulling the pin straight down and snugly against the fabric. This pin is temporary and prevents fabrics from shifting during pin placement; do not tilt the pin at all, as doing so may cause the fabric to shift. Now, place a pin ¹⁄₁₆" (1.5 mm) from the pin marking the intersection point, to both the left and right of it. Remove the pin marking the intersection point before starting to stitch the seam line.

To Sew a Quilt Top

1. Sew two blocks together and press.

2. Continue sewing blocks together, pressing after each block is added, until a row is complete.

3. Sew rows together, pressing after the addition of each row, until the quilt top is assembled.

Do not sew over pins, as striking a pin with the machine needle can break or dull the needle, damage your machine, and place undue wear on the feed dogs.

Pressing

Properly pressed seams make it easier to match seams and piece accurately.

- Set your iron to the highest temperature setting the fabric fiber content will allow. Typically this is the cotton setting.

- Use a firm pressing surface. If the ironing surface is too padded, it is easier to distort a quilt block.

- Set a seam by pressing from the wrong side of the fabric before pressing it open or to one side, especially for long fabric strips. Then, open the seam and press in the desired direction. Pressing the seam flat and then open sharpens the seam line and makes matching seams easier.

- Press using a downward motion. Unlike ironing, which involves moving an iron across fabric, pressing a seam involves moving the iron down on the seam. If you iron across a unit, you may unwittingly distort it, and the unit may bow or curve.

- Press seams from the right side of the fabric toward the darker fabric, unless there is a reason to do otherwise. Reasons for not pressing toward a dark fabric include: reducing bulk, and/or creating opposing seams so that when a unit is pieced to a neighboring seam, the seams go in opposing directions and "nest" together (see photo at left).

Placing a portable pressing surface next to your sewing machine makes it easier to press each seam after sewing.

- Avoid pressing a bias seam (fabric cut on the diagonal of the selvage) unit until it is stitched to another patch of fabric; use your fingernail to gently press delicate bias seams instead.

- If your finished block is not perfectly square, block it with a piece of freezer paper. Fabric is somewhat fluid, and it is possible to manipulate it into the desired shape. Cut a piece of freezer paper to the unfinished size of the block. Press the waxy side of the freezer paper onto the ironing board. Pin the corners of the block to match the corners of the freezer paper, and use starch and a hot steam iron to coax the block into shape.

- When four or more seams come together, press the seams open by putting a dab of water in the center of the seam intersections and pressing. This helps the bulky seam intersection lie flat and distributes the bulk of the seam evenly.

- Using steam while pressing can distort quilt blocks. If using steam, let the quilt unit cool and dry completely before removing it from the ironing surface. Doing so minimizes unwanted distortion or stretching out of shape.

Quilt Layouts

There are several popular ways to arrange blocks, including horizontal, on-point, and in strips.

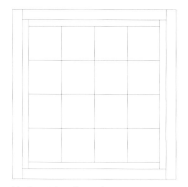

Horizontal quilt setting

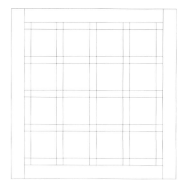

Horizontal quilt setting with sashing

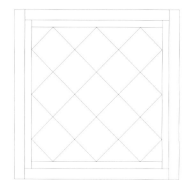

On-point quilt setting

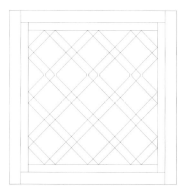

On-point quilt setting with sashing

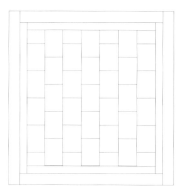

Vertical strip quilt layout

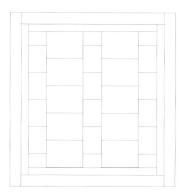

Vertical strip quilt layout with varying widths

1 | Counterpane

Skill Level: Intermediate

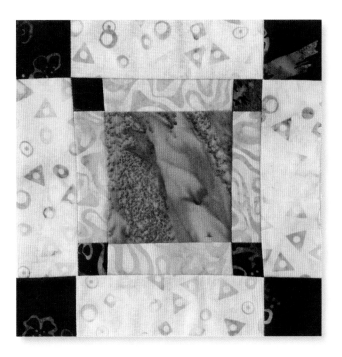

(continued)

Cutting Instructions for One Block

Unit	Quantity	6" (15.2 cm) Finished	9" (22.9 cm) Finished	12" (30.5 cm) Finished
A	4	1½" × 1½" (3.8 × 3.8 cm)	2" × 2" (5.1 × 5.1 cm)	2½" × 2½" (6.4 × 6.4 cm)
B	4	1½" × 4½" (3.8 × 11.4 cm)	2" × 6½" (5.1 × 16.5 cm)	2½" × 8½" (6.4 × 21.6 cm)
C	4	1⅛" × 1⅛" (2.9 × 2.9 cm)	1½" × 1½" (3.8 × 3.8 cm)	1⅞" × 1⅞" (4.8 × 4.8 cm)
D	4	1⅛" × 3⅛" (2.9 × 7.9 cm)	1½" × 4½" (3.8 × 11.4 cm)	1⅞" × 5⅞" (4.8 × 14.9 cm)
E	1	3⅛" × 3⅛" (7.9 × 7.9 cm)	4½" × 4½" (11.4 × 11.4 cm)	5⅞" × 5⅞" (14.9 × 14.9 cm)

Piecing Instructions

1. Stitch a C square unit to opposing sides of a D rectangle unit to make a C-D-C unit. Press seam allowance toward C. Make 2.

2. Sew a D rectangle unit to opposing sides of the E square unit to make a D-E-D unit. Press seam allowance toward E. Make 1.

3. Stitch an A square unit to opposing sides of a B rectangle unit to make an A-B-A unit. Press toward A. Make 2.

4. Stitch the C-D-C unit to the top and bottom of the D-E-D unit. Seams should nest, or go in opposite directions, thereby making it easier to match the seam intersections. Press toward E.

5. Stitch a B rectangle unit to opposing sides of the unit created in step 4. Press toward D.

6. Stitch the A-B-A unit to the top and bottom sides of the unit created in step 5. Press toward B.

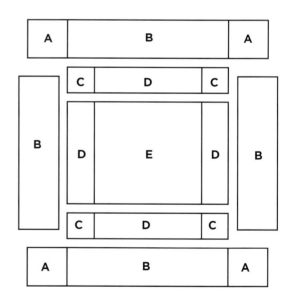

2 | Rail Fence Gone Modern

Skill Level: Beginner

What gives this quilt block movement is a combination of light, medium, and dark fabrics. For a striking result, gradate the fabrics from light to dark as you sew the rectangle patches together to make the block. Alternatively, for a scrappy look, use a wide variety of fabrics.

The inspiration for this block is a common pattern known as Rail Fence. By layering two of these blocks, stitching them together, and cutting them apart, a fresh, modern block emerges.

(continued)

Cutting Instructions for One Block

Unit	Quantity	6" (15.24 cm) Finished	9" (23 cm) Finished	12" (30 cm) Finished
A	4	2" × 6½" (5 × 16.5 cm)	2¾" × 9½" (7 × 24.25 cm)	3½" × 12½" (8.75 × 31.75 cm)

Piecing Instructions

1. Stitch the A rectangle units together to make a block. Press all the seams in the same direction. Make 2.

2. Lay two blocks that contrast in color on top of each other, right sides together, with the seams running vertically. On the wrong side of the fabric, use a mechanical pencil to mark a diagonal line from the top left corner to the bottom right corner.

3. Stitch a ¼" (6 mm) away from each side of the marked line.

4. Using a rotary cutter and ruler, cut on the *marked* line, creating two blocks. Press the seam allowance in either direction.

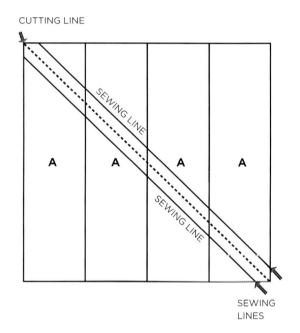

CUTTING LINE

SEWING LINE

A   A   A   A

SEWING LINE

SEWING LINES

3 | Hand Weave

Skill Level: Intermediate

Consider cutting four of the B units in the same fabric as the D unit, and cut the remaining four B units in a different fabric. This adds visual interest to the block, and gives the illusion of a square behind a square.

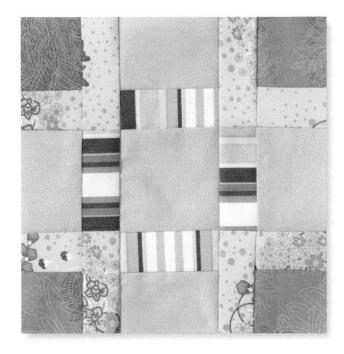

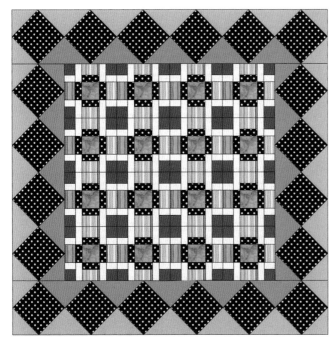

(continued)

Cutting Instructions for One Block

Unit	Quantity	6" (15.24 cm) Finished	9" (23 cm) Finished	12" (30 cm) Finished
A	4	1¾" × 1¾" (4.5 cm × 4.5 cm)	2⅜" × 2⅜" (6 cm × 6 cm)	3" × 3" (7.5 cm × 7.5 cm)
B	4—Color 1 14—Color 2	1¼" × 2½" (3.25 × 6.25 cm)	1⅝" × 3½" (3.75 × 8.75 cm)	2" × 4½" (5 × 11.25 cm)
C	4	1¾" × 2½" (4.5 × 6.25 cm)	2⅜" × 3½" (6 × 8.75 cm)	3" × 4½" (7.5 × 11.25 cm)
D	4—Color 1	1¼" × 1¾" (3.25 × 4.5 cm)	1⅝" × 2⅜" (3.75 × 6 cm)	2" × 3" (5 × 7.5 cm)
E	1	2½" × 2½" (6.25 × 6.25 cm)	3½" × 3½" (8.75 × 8.75 cm)	4½" × 4½" (11.25 × 11.25 cm)

Piecing Instructions

1. Stitch the A square unit to the D rectangle unit to make an A-D unit. Press the seam allowance toward the D unit. Make 4.

2. Stitch the A-D unit to the B rectangle (color 1) unit to make an A-D-B unit. Press the seam allowance toward the B unit. Make 4.

3. Stitch the B rectangle unit (color 2) to the C rectangle unit to make a B-C unit. Make 4.

4. Stitch an A-D-B unit to opposing sides of a B-C unit to make the top row of the block. Press toward the A-D-B unit. Repeat to create the bottom row of the block.

5. To create the center row of the block, stitch a C-B unit to opposing sides of an E square unit. Press toward the E unit.

6. Following the piecing diagram, sew the three rows together to complete the block. Seams should nest, or go in opposite directions, thereby making it easier to match the seam intersections. Press the seam allowance toward the top row and bottom row.

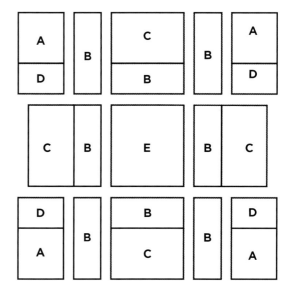

4 | Chuck-A-Luck

Skill Level: Beginner

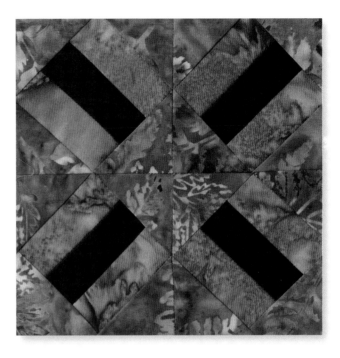

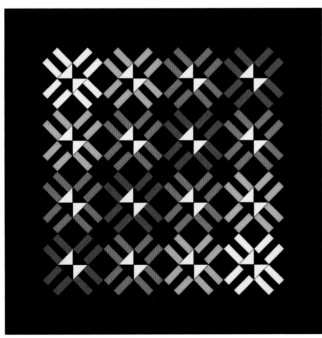

(continued)

Cutting Instructions for One Block

Unit	Subcut	Quantity	6" (15.24 cm) Finished	9" (23 cm) Finished	12" (30 cm) Finished
A	 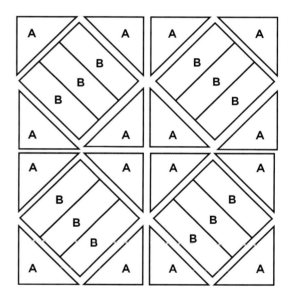	16	2⅜" × 2⅜" (6 × 6 cm)	3⅛" × 3⅛" (8 × 8 cm)	3⅞" × 3⅞" (9.75 × 9.75 cm)
B		8—Color 1 14—Color 2	1¼" × 2⅝" (3.25 × 6.5 cm)	1½" × 3⅝" (3.75 × 9 cm)	1⅞" × 4¾" (4.75 × 12 cm)

Piecing Instructions

1. Stitch a B rectangle unit (color 1) to each side of a B rectangle unit (color 2) to make a B-B-B unit. Make 4.

2. Stitch an A triangle to each side of the B-B-B unit. Press toward the A unit. Make 4.

3. Stitch two of the units created in step 2 together to make a row. Pay attention to the orientation of the units before you sew them together, as it is easy to turn the unit in the wrong direction. Refer to the piecing diagram to see the correct orientation. Press the seams open. Make two.

4. Stitch together the two rows created in step 3. Pay attention to the orientation of the rows before you sew them together, as it is easy to have the rows reversed. Refer to the piecing diagram to see the correct orientation. Press the seam open.

5 | Stripes Inside

Skill Level: Beginner

This block is versatile and makes an excellent pieced border as well.

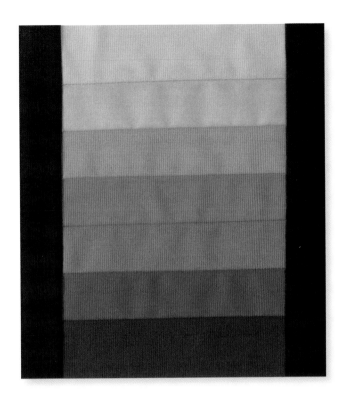

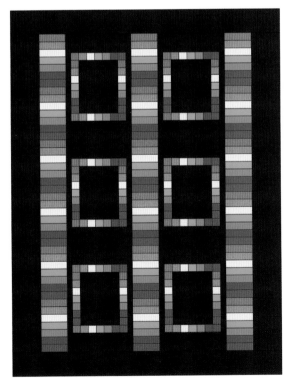

This quilt layout combines two blocks: Stripes Inside and Stripes Outside (page 27). The setting is a horizontal strip layout, and the rows of strips alternate in width. The rows with the Stripes Inside blocks are six inches, while the rows with the Stripes Outside blocks are nine inches. This adds a level of visual interest and complexity to the quilt.

(continued)

Cutting Instructions for One Block

Unit	Quantity	6" (15.24 cm) Finished	9" (23 cm) Finished	12" (30 cm) Finished
A	2	1⅜" × 6½" (3.5 × 16.5 cm)	1¾" × 9½" (4.5 × 24.25 cm)	2¼" × 12½" (5.75 × 31.75 cm)
B	7	1⅜" × 4¾" (3.5 × 12 cm)	1¾" × 6⅞" (4.5 × 17.5 cm)	2¼" × 9⅛" (5.75 × 23.25 cm)

Piecing Instructions

1. Stitch the B rectangle units together, pressing the seams in one direction.

2. Stitch an A rectangle unit to opposing sides of the unit created in step 1. Press the seams toward A.

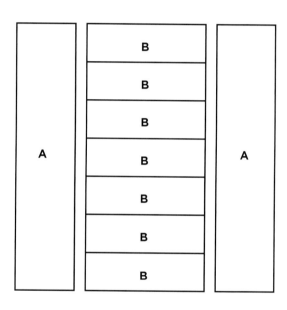

6 | Stripes Outside

Skill Level: Beginner

This block is versatile and makes an excellent border as well.

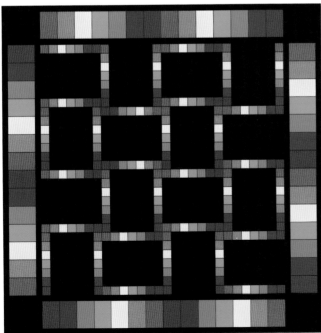

This quilt layout combines two blocks: Stripes Inside (page 25) and Stripes Outside. The quilt interior uses Stripes Outside blocks, while the border uses Stripes Inside blocks.

(continued)

Cutting Instructions for One Block

Unit	Quantity	6" (15.24 cm) Finished	9" (23 cm) Finished	12" (30 cm) Finished
A	14	1⅜" × 1⅜" (3.5 × 3.5 cm)	1¾" × 1¾" (4.5 × 4.5 cm)	2¼" × 2¼" (4.25 × 4.25 cm)
B	1	4¾" × 6½" (12 × 16.5 cm)	6⅞" × 9½" (17.5 × 24.25 cm)	9⅛" × 12½" (23.25 × 31.75 cm)

Piecing Instructions

1. Stitch the A square units together, pressing the seams in one direction.

2. Stitch the result of step 1 to opposing sides of a B rectangle unit.

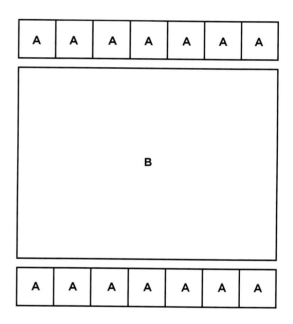

7 | Storm at Sea

Skill Level: Advanced

This block has broad appeal, and can appear quite different based on the colors selected for the units of the block. With different colorations, a wave, curved shapes, a heart, or stars emerge.

(continued)

Cutting Instructions for One Block

Unit	Sub-cut	Quantity	6" (15.24 cm) Finished	9" (23 cm) Finished	12" (30 cm) Finished
A		16—Color 1 4—Color 2	1⅝" × 1⅝" (3.75 cm × 3.75 cm)	2" × 2" (5 cm × 5 cm)	2⅜" × 2⅜" (6 × 6 cm)
B	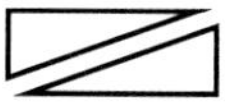	8	1⅜" × 2¾" (3.5 × 7 cm)	1¾" × 3½" (4.5 × 8.75 cm)	2⅛" × 4¼" (5.25 × 10.75 cm)
C	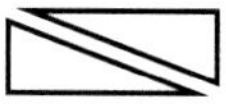	8	1⅜" × 2¾" (3.5 × 7 cm)	1¾" × 3½" (4.5 × 8.75 cm)	2⅛" × 4¼" (5.25 × 10.75 cm)
D		4	2⅜" × 2⅜" (6 × 6 cm)	3⅛" × 3⅛"(8 × 8 cm)	3⅞" × 3⅞" (9.75 × 9.75 cm)
E*	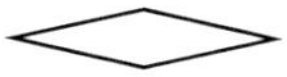	4	1⅞" × 2¼" (4.75 × 5.75 cm)	2½" × 3⅛" (6.25 × 8 cm)	3⅛" × 4" (8 × 10 cm)
F		4	2¾" × 2¾" (7 × 7 cm)	3½" × 3½" (8.75 × 8.75 cm)	4¼" × 4¼" (10.75 × 10.75 cm)
G		1	1½" × 1½" (3.75 × 3.75 cm)	2⅛" × 2⅛" (5.25 × 5.25 cm)	2⅝" × 2⅝" (6.5 cm × 6.5 cm)
H		16	2" × 2" (5 × 5 cm)	2⅜" × 2⅜" (6 × 6 cm)	2¾" × 2¾" (7 × 7 cm)
I		4	1" × 1" (2.5 × 2.5 cm)	1¼" × 1¼" (3.25 × 3.25 cm)	1½" × 1½" (3.75 × 3.75 cm)
J		16	1¼" × 1¼" (3.25 × 3.25 cm)	1⅜" × 1⅜" (3.5 × 3.5 cm)	1⅝" × 1⅝" (4 × 4 cm)

*Note: For unit E, there is a template on the following page to assist in cutting the sharp angles of the unit. Place the template on the fabric, and cut on the dotted lines.

Piecing Instructions

1. Stitch the J triangle units to each side of the I square unit. Press toward J. Make 4.

2. Stitch an H triangle unit to each side of the outcome from step 1. Press toward H. Make 4.

3. Stitch an A triangle unit to each side of the outcome from step 2 to make an I-J-H-A unit. Press toward A. Make 4.

4. Stitch a C triangle unit to opposing sides of the E diamond unit to make a C-E unit. Press toward C. Make 4.

5. Stitch a B triangle unit to opposing sides of the C-E unit to make a B-C-E unit. Press toward B. Make 4.

6. Repeat steps 1–3 to make the center G-A-F-D unit.

7. Stitch an I-J-H-A unit to opposing sides of a B-C-E unit to make rows 1 and 3. Press toward the B-C-E unit.

8. Stitch a B-C-E unit to opposing sides of the G-A-F-D unit to make row 2. Press toward the B-C-E unit.

9. Stitch rows 1, 2, and 3 together.

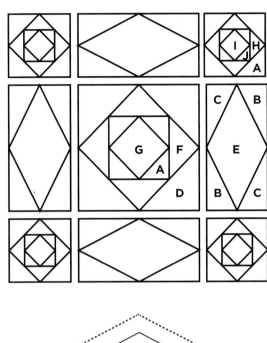

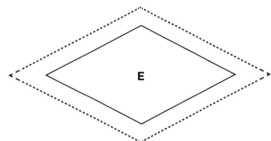

8 | Rolling Stone Twisted

Skill Level: Beginner

This block is based on a traditional block from the 1920s known as Rolling Stone. By cutting this block apart and re-assembling it, a contemporary counterpart emerges.

This quilt layout combines two blocks: Rolling Stone-Twisted and Counterpane (page 17).

Cutting Instructions for One Block

Unit	Sub-cut	Quantity	6" (15.24 cm) Finished	9" (23 cm) Finished	12" (30 cm) Finished
A	 ◩	16	1⅞" × 1⅞" (4.75 × 4.75 cm)	2⅜" × 2⅜" (6 × 6 cm)	2⅞" × 2⅞" (7.25 × 7.25 cm)
B		4—Color 1 4—Color 2	1⅝" × 2⅝" (4 × 6.5 cm)	2⅛" × 3⅝" (5.25 × 9 cm)	2⅝" × 4⅝" (6.5 × 11.5 cm)
C		1	2⅝" × 2⅝" (6.5 × 6.5 cm)	3⅝" × 3⅝" (9 × 9 cm)	4⅝" × 4⅝" (11.5 × 11.5 cm)
D		4	2" × 2" (5 × 5 cm)	2¾" × 2¾" (7 × 7 cm)	3½" × 3½" (8.75 × 8.75 cm)

Piecing Instructions

1. Stitch an A triangle unit to each side of D square unit to make an A-D unit. Press toward A. Make 4.

2. Stitch a B rectangle unit (color 1) to a B rectangle unit (color 2) to make a B-B unit. Make 4.

3. Stitch an A-D unit to opposing sides of the B-B unit to make rows 1 and 3. Press toward A-D. Make 2.

4. Stitch a B-B unit to opposing sides of the C square unit to make row 2. Press toward C.

5. Stitch rows 1, 2, and 3.

6. Using a rotary cutter and ruler, cut the block into fourths, creating units A, B, C, and D.

7. Rotate units B and C. Stitch units A and B together to form row 1. Stitch units C and D together to form row 2. Sew rows 1 and 2 together.

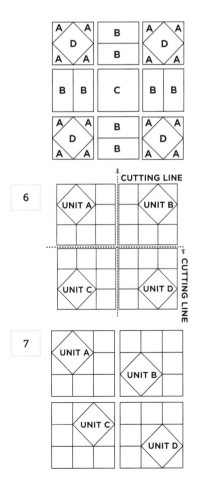

9 | Arrowhead Puzzle

Skill Level: Intermediate

This block was inspired by a traditional block known as Arrowhead Puzzle. While this version is simplified, it is very close to the original version.

Cutting Instructions for One Block

Unit	Sub-cut	Quantity	6" (15.24 cm) Finished	9" (23 cm) Finished	12" (30 cm) Finished
A		4—Color 1 4—Color 2	2¾" × 2¾" (7 × 7 cm)	3½" × 3½" (8.75 × 8.75 cm)	4¼" × 4¼" (10.75 × 10.75 cm)
B		2—Color 1 2—Color 2 2—Color 3 2—Color 4	2⅜" × 2⅜" (6 × 6 cm)	3⅛" × 3⅛" (8 × 8 cm)	3⅞" × 3⅞" (9.75 × 9.75 cm)
C		4	2⅝" × 2⅝" (6.5 × 6.5 cm)	3⅝" × 3⅝" (9 × 9 cm)	4¾" × 4¾" (12 × 12 cm)
D		2—Color 1 2—Color 2	1½" × 1½" (3.75 × 3.75 cm)	2⅛" × 2⅛" (5.25 × 5.25 cm)	2⅝" × 2⅝" (6.5 × 6.5 cm)

Piecing Instructions

1. Stitch two A triangle units together (color 1 and color 2), to make an A-A unit. Make 2 with color 1 on the right-hand side of the A-A unit, and make 2 with color 1 on the left-hand side of the A-A unit.

2. Stitch the two B triangle units together (color 1) to make a B-B unit. Repeat for the other three colors to make four B-B units.

3. Stitch an A-A unit to one side of a C square unit to make an A-A-C unit. Make 4.

4. Stitch a B-B unit to opposing sides of an A-A-C unit. Make 2.

5. Stitch two D square units together (color 1 and color 2) to make a D-D unit. Make 2. Join the two D-D units together.

6. Stitch an A-A-C unit to opposing sides of the outcome of step 5.

7. Stitch the three rows together.

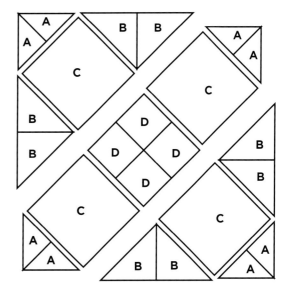

10 | Squares upon Squares

Skill Level: Beginner

With proper color placement, this block gives the illusion of the center block transparently sitting upon the square in the background. In the block shown, the yellow appears to sit transparently over the blue, turning the shared corner green.

This quilt layout combines two blocks. The interior of the quilt uses Squares Upon Squares blocks set on-point. The border of the quilt uses the Stripes Bordered Outside block (page 38).

Cutting Instructions for One Block

Unit	Quantity	6" (15.24 cm) Finished	9" (23 cm) Finished	12" (30 cm) Finished
A	1—Color 1 2—Color 2	2" × 3½" (5 × 8.75 cm)	2¾" × 5" (7 × 12.75 cm)	3½" × 6½" (8.75 × 16.5 cm)
B	2—Color 1 1—Color 2 1—Color 3 2—Color 4	2" × 2" (5 × 5 cm)	2¾" × 2¾" (7 × 7 cm)	3½" × 3½" (8.75 × 8.75 cm)
C	1	3½" × 3½" (8.75 × 8.75 cm)	5" × 5" (12.75 × 12.75 cm)	6½" × 6½" (16.5 × 16.5 cm)

Piecing Instructions

1. Stitch two B square units together, to make a B-B unit. Make 3.

2. Stitch an A rectangle unit to a B-B unit to make an A-B-B unit. Make 3.

3. Stitch two A-B-B square units together to make row 1.

4. Stitch an A-B-B square unit to a C square unit to make row 2.

5. Stitch the two rows together.

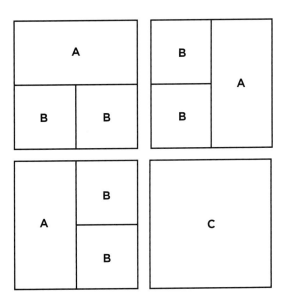

11 | Stripes Bordered Outside

Skill Level: Beginner

This versatile block also makes
an excellent pieced border.

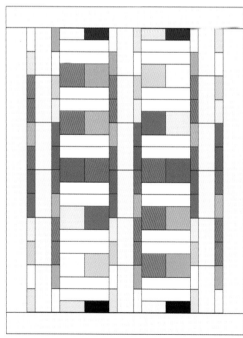

Cutting Instructions for One Block

Unit	Quantity	6" (15.24 cm) Finished	9" (23 cm) Finished	12" (30 cm) Finished
A	2	2" × 6½" (5 × 16.5 cm)	2¾" × 9½" (7 × 24.25 cm)	3½" × 12½" (8.75 × 31.75 cm)
B	1—Color 1 1—Color 2	3½" × 3½" (8.75 × 8.75 cm)	5" × 5" (12.75 × 12.75 cm)	6½" × 6½" (16.5 × 16.5 cm)

Piecing Instructions

1. Stitch two B square units together, to make a B-B unit.

2. Stitch an A rectangle unit to opposing sides of a B-B unit.

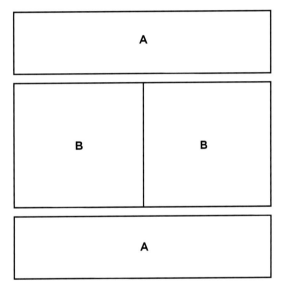

12 | Stripes Bordered Inside

Skill Level: Beginner

This versatile block also makes an
excellent pieced border.

Cutting Instructions for One Block

Unit	Quantity	6" (15.24 cm) Finished	9" (23 cm) Finished	12" (30 cm) Finished
A	1—Color 1 1—Color 2 1—Color 3 1—Color 4	2" × 3½" (5 × 8.75 cm)	2¾" × 5" (7 × 12.75 cm)	3½" × 6½" (8.75 × 16.5 cm)
B	1	3½" × 6½" (8.75 × 16.5 cm)	5" × 9½" (12.75 × 24.25 cm)	6½" × 12½" (16.5 × 31.75 cm)

Piecing Instructions

1. Stitch two A rectangle units together, to make an A-A unit. Make 2.

2. Stitch an A-A unit to opposing sides of a B rectangle unit.

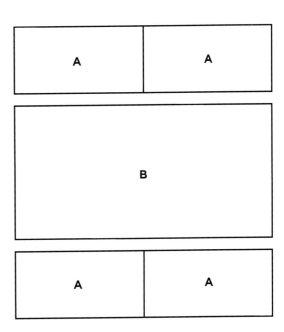

13 | Walls of Jericho

Skill Level: Beginner

Cutting Instructions for One Block

Unit	Sub-cut	Quantity	6" (15.24 cm) Finished	9" (23 cm) Finished	12" (30 cm) Finished
A		2	3⅝" × 3⅝" (9 × 9 cm)	5" × 5" (12.75 × 12.75 cm)	6⅜" × 6⅜" (16.25 × 16.25 cm)
B		1	1" × 6½" (2.5 × 16.5 cm)	1¼" × 9½" (3.25 × 24.25 cm)	1½" × 12½" (3.75 × 31.75 cm)
C		2	1" × 3¼" (2.5 × 8.25 cm)	1¼" × 4⅝" (3.25 × 11.5 cm)	1½" × 6" (3.75 × 15.25 cm)
D*		4	1⅜" × 5⅛" (3.5 × 13 cm)	1⅞" × 7" (4.75 × 17.75 cm)	2¼" × 9" (5.75 × 23 cm)
E		4	2⅜" × 2⅜" (6 × 6 cm)	3⅛" × 3⅛" (8 × 8 cm)	3⅞" × 3⅞" (9.75 × 9.75 cm)

* Note: For unit D, cut the rectangle, then use a quilting ruler to cut the ends at 45° to make a trapezoid.

Piecing Instructions

1. Stitch a triangle A unit to a D unit to make an A-D unit. Make 4.

2. Stitch an E triangle unit to an A-D unit to make an A-D-E unit. Make 4.

3. Stitch an A-D-E unit to opposing sides of a C rectangle unit. Make 2.

4. Stitch the outcome of step 3 to opposing sides of a B rectangle unit to complete the block.

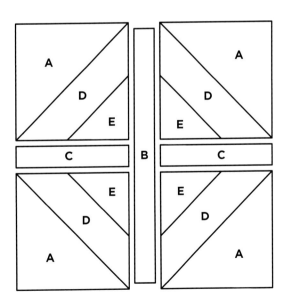

14 | Tea Leaf

Skill Level: Beginner

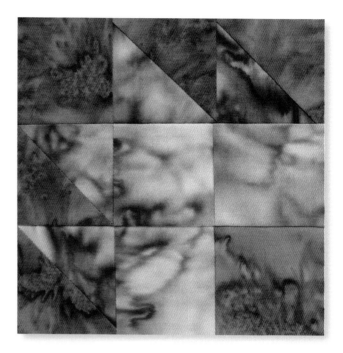

Cutting Instructions for One Block

Unit	Sub-cut	Quantity	6" (15.24 cm) Finished	9" (23 cm) Finished	12" (30 cm) Finished
A		1—Color 1 1—Color 2 3—Color 3	2½" × 2½" (6.25 × 6.25 cm)	3½" × 3½" (8.75 × 8.75 cm)	4½" × 4½" (11.25 × 11.25 cm)
B	◩	2—Color 1 2—Color 2	2⅞" × 2⅞" (7.25 × 7.25 cm)	3⅞" × 3⅞" (9.75 × 9.75 cm)	4⅞" × 4⅞" (12.25 × 12.25 cm)

Piecing Instructions

1. Stitch two B triangle units together to make a B-B unit. Make 4.

2. Stitch two A square units together to make an A-A unit. Make 2.

3. Stitch two B-B units together to make a B-B-B-B unit. Make 2.

4. Stitch two A-A units together to make an A-A-A-A unit. Make 1.

5. Stitch a B-B-B-B unit to one side of the A-A-A-A unit.

6. Stitch an A square unit to one of the B-B-B-B units.

7. Stitch the outcome of step 5 and the outcome of step 6 together to complete the block.

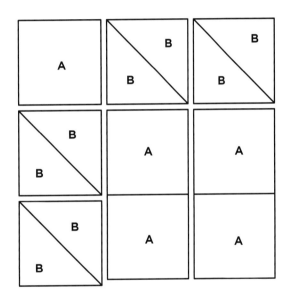

15 | Bright Hopes

Skill Level: Intermediate

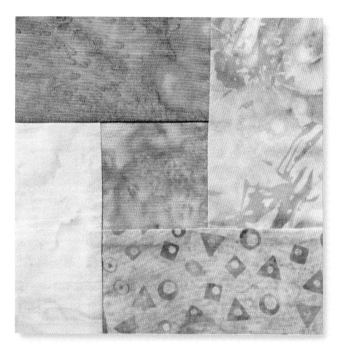

Cutting Instructions for One Block

Unit	Quantity	6" (15.24 cm) Finished	9" (23 cm) Finished	12" (30 cm) Finished
A	1—Color 1 1—Color 2 1—Color 3 1—Color 4	2½" × 4½" (6.25 × 11.25 cm)	3½" × 6½" (8.75 × 16.5 cm)	4½" × 8½" (11.25 × 21.25 cm)
B	1	2½" × 2½" (6.25 × 6.25 cm)	3½" × 3½" (8.75 × 8.75 cm)	4½" × 4½" (11.25 × 11.25 cm)

Piecing Instructions

1. Stitch the rectangle unit A(1) to the square B unit with a partial seam. Do not sew to the edge of the square B unit. Press the seam toward the A(1) unit.

2. Stitch the rectangle unit A(2) to the square B unit with a partial seam. Do not sew to the edge of the square B unit. Press the seam toward the A(2) unit.

3. Finish sewing the remainder of the A(1) partial seam.

4. Stitch the rectangle unit A(3) to the square B unit with a partial seam. Do not sew to the edge of the square B unit. Press the seam toward the A(3) unit.

5. Finish sewing the remainder of the A(2) partial seam.

6. Stitch the rectangle unit A(4) to the square B unit with a partial seam. Do not sew to the edge of the square B unit. Press the seam toward the A(4) unit.

7. Finish sewing the remainder of the A(3) partial seam.

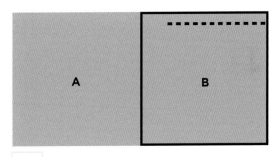

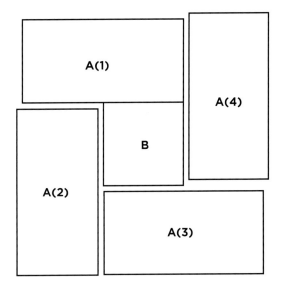

16 | Scotch Quilt

Skill Level: Intermediate

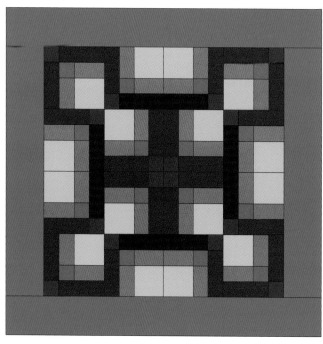

Cutting Instructions for One Block

Unit	Quantity	6" (15.24 cm) Finished	9" (23 cm) Finished	12" (30 cm) Finished
A	2	2" × 5" (5 × 12.75 cm)	2¾" × 7¼" (7 × 18.4 cm)	3½" × 9½" (8.75 × 24.1 cm)
B	1	2" × 2" (5 × 5 cm)	2¾" × 2¾" (7 × 7 cm)	3½" × 3½" (8.75 × 8.75 cm)
C	2	2" × 3½" (5 × 8.75 cm)	2¾" × 5" (7 × 12.75 cm)	3½" × 6½" (8.75 × 16.5 cm)
D	1	3½" × 3½" (8.75 × 8.75 cm)	5" × 5" (12.75 × 12.75 cm)	6½" × 6½" (16.5 cm × 16.5 cm)

Piecing Instructions

1. Stitch the D square unit to a C rectangle unit to make an A-D unit. Press toward D.

2. Stitch a C rectangle unit to a B square unit to make a B-C unit. Press toward B.

3. Stitch a B square unit to an A rectangle unit to make an A-B unit. Press toward A.

4. Stitch the C-D unit to the B-C unit.

5. Stitch an A rectangle unit to the outcome of step 4. Press toward A.

6. Stitch the A-B unit to the outcome of step 5.

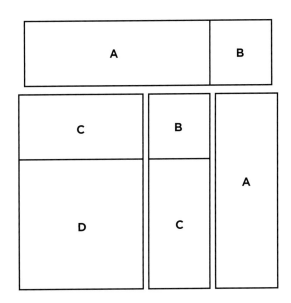

17 | Flutter Wheel

Skill Level: Intermediate

This quilt layout combines two blocks:
Flutter Wheel and Dakota Star (page 76).

Cutting Instructions for One Block

Unit	Sub-cut	Quantity	6" (15.24 cm) Finished	9" (23 cm) Finished	12" (30 cm) Finished
A	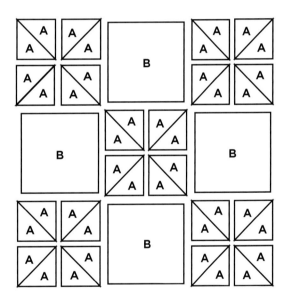	10—Color 1 2—Color 2 2—Color 3 2—Color 4 2—Color 5 2—Color 6	1⅞" × 1⅞" (4.75 × 4.75 cm)	2⅜" × 2⅜" (6 × 6 cm)	2⅞" × 2⅞" (7.25 × 7.25 cm)
B		4	2½" × 2½" (6.25 × 6.25 cm)	3½" × 3½" (8.75 × 8.75 cm)	4½" × 4½" (11.25 × 11.25 cm)

Piecing Instructions

1. Stitch two A triangle units together to make an A-A unit. Make 20.

2. Stitch two A-A units together to make an A-A-A-A unit. Make 10.

3. Stitch two A-A-A-A triangle units together to make a pinwheel block. Make 5.

4. Stitch two pinwheel blocks to opposing sides of a B square unit for row 1. Repeat for row 3.

5. Stitch two B square units to opposing sides of a pinwheel block for row 2. Stitch rows one, two, and three together to complete the block.

Foundation-Pieced Blocks

Foundation piecing (also called paper piecing) offers the opportunity to construct unbelievably narrow points, control bias edges, and use teeny-tiny pieces of fabric. With this method, slippery or unusual fabrics are easy to incorporate. In addition, it offers incredible precision and accuracy: all the blocks are always the same size. For foundation piecing, fabric pieces are roughly cut for each numbered section of a paper pattern. Translucent foundation paper allows you to see through it as pieces are stitched together from the wrong side of the paper through the pattern lines, one piece at a time in numbered sequence.

Tools and Supplies

Foundation piecing requires many of the same tools used for traditional piecing, as well as some specialized tools. These specialized tools include the following:

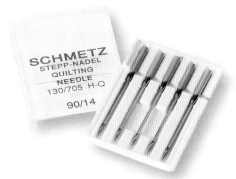

Foundation paper: Use translucent paper (such as tracing paper or vellum) to trace or copy the foundation pattern. Quilt shops also carry foundation paper that is lightweight and similar to newsprint. You can also use copier or parchment paper. The best paper is lightweight and tears easily from the stitched line.

Paper or template plastic: Use paper or plastic templates to pre-cut the units in the foundation-pieced block.

Temporary double-stick tape: Adhere the template to the fabric to prevent the template from slipping when you cut the fabric units.

Washable fabric glue stick: Use the glue stick to adhere the first unit onto the back of the foundation pattern. This will prevent the patch from slipping before you sew the first seam.

Presser foot: Select a foot suitable for straight stitching. The best options have a mark in the center of the foot, making it easier to follow the stitching line on the paper. A foot with a clear sole or an open toe foot offer best visibility.

Sewing machine needle: Use a slightly larger needle than those used for traditional piecing. I suggest a 90/14 sharp or quilting needle, as the larger holes do a better job of perforating the paper, making it easier to remove the paper after sewing.

Folding Template: Cut a 3" × 11" (7.5 × 28 cm) piece from tagboard, template plastic, or card stock. A folding template has a thin, straight edge used for creasing seamlines in the foundation pattern before stitching them.

Add-A-Quarter Ruler from CM Designs: Available in most quilt shops in 6," 12," or 18" [15.3, 30.5, or 45.8 cm] lengths, this ruler has a ¼" (6 mm) lip on the right side. The 12-inch (30.5 cm) ruler is the most versatile. For foundation piecing, this ruler aids in trimming seam allowance to ¼" (6 mm) after stitching each piece.

Tweezers: Tweezers are useful for removing stray paper bits when separating the paper foundation from the block after sewing. too thick and prevent the seam from lying flat while sewing.

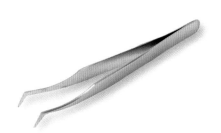

General Cutting Instructions

Asymmetrical shapes and triangles are difficult to cut correctly. While it is possible to foundation piece without using templates, the process is made far simpler by pre-cutting rough shapes that are large enough and have the proper angle to cover the foundation.

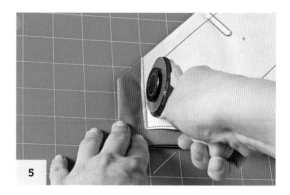

5

When foundation piecing, always sew on the underside of the paper, *not* on the side of the paper with the drawn pattern. To prevent reversing the image, place the templates on the wrong side of the fabric when cutting the fabric units.

Cutting with Template

1. Print the foundation piecing cutting templates on regular printer paper. The templates include a ½" (12 mm) seam allowance to allow some forgiveness when placing the fabric on the foundation.

2. Cut out the paper templates. You do not have to cut precisely on the line; cutting the templates roughly around the dashed line is preferable. Just focus on trimming any excess paper away and cutting the templates apart from each other.

3. Layer one to six layers of fabric with wrong sides facing up.

4. Place a piece of temporary double-stick tape on the back of the paper template. Place the template on the wrong side of the fabric, aligning the grainline arrow with either the lengthwise or crosswise grain of the fabric.

5. Cut on the dotted. Unless otherwise noted in the cutting instructions for the block, it is acceptable to use the templates to roughly cut out the fabric units. Cutting precisely on the dotted line is not necessary, but DO NOT cut the units any smaller than the dotted line. If you find it easier, use a rotary cutter and ruler to help cut out the shapes by aligning the edge of the ruler with the dashed line of the template. For additional tips and instruction on using a rotary cutter and ruler, refer to the rotary cutting details in the Piecing Basics section of the book.

After cutting a fabric shape for the foundation block, paper clip the template and fabric stack together. This helps you stay organized and ensures that you will use the properly labeled units when constructing the block.

Transferring the Pattern to Foundation Paper

Using one of the techniques described below, copy the foundation pattern. Make a paper pattern for each block you want to make. For example, if you want to make a quilt with twenty-four blocks, you will need to copy the pattern twenty-four times. Moreover, making an extra copy or two is a good idea, in the event that you make a mistake. Test different papers to see which kind you prefer. Remember that with foundation piecing, the finished block will be a mirror image of the paper pattern, since the fabric is on the underside of the paper when you are sewing from the topside (printed side) of the paper.

Photocopier / Printer

Use a copier to transfer the foundation pattern with discretion. While it is an easy way to transfer multiple copies of a pattern, all copiers and printers distort a pattern in at least one direction. This creates an inaccurate block, which negates one of the prime benefits of foundation piecing. The patterns provided in the book measure 6" (15.24 cm) finished, and 6½" (16.5 cm) unfinished. When checking a copied image for accuracy, check both the width and height of the duplicated image.

If using a copier to transfer the foundation pattern, verify the accuracy of the printed block before stitching. In addition, verify that the settings of the copier are:

• No scaling

• Actual Size or scaling of 100%

• If the copier machine has "Fit to Frame" setting selected, it will enlarge or reduce the pattern to fit the page. DO NOT select "Fit to Frame", as this option is inaccurate.

Tracing

This method is the most accurate and simplest way of duplicating the foundation pattern. Trace the pattern with a pencil and ruler onto the foundation material (such as tracing paper, vellum, newsprint, or copy paper).

(continued)

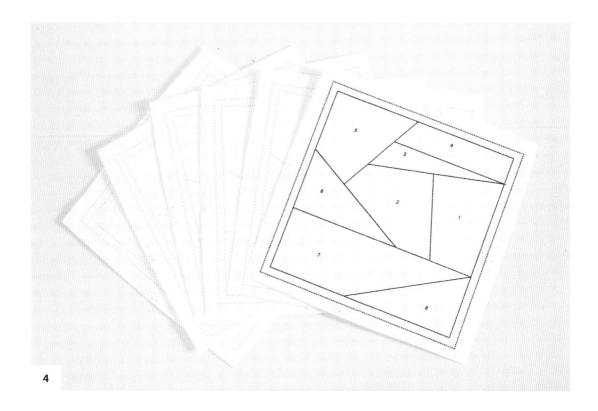

4

Needle Punching

This method of duplicating the foundation pattern has the added benefit of pre-perforating the patterns, making removal of the foundation at the end of the process that much easier. To needle-punch several patterns at once:

1. Trace the pattern onto the desired foundation material.

2. Stack 5–7 pieces of foundation material together, placing the traced pattern on top of the stack, and staple the stack together to prevent shifting.

3. Remove the top thread from your sewing machine, increase the stitch length of the machine to 8–10 stitches per inch (2.5–3.0 mm), and stitch on the line of the foundation pattern. Since the machine is unthreaded, this action needle punches the entire stack of paper foundations with the pattern. If your machine has an upper thread sensor to alert you the upper thread is broken, deactivate the upper thread sensor in the settings of your machine before attempting this method, or the machine will stop to alert you that the thread is broken every few stitches.

4. Remove the staples from the stack of foundation patterns and separate the foundation patterns to reveal the needle-punched pattern. To guide you as you stitch, hand write the pattern numbers on the foundations (as shown on the master pattern).

General Piecing Instructions

When piecing on a temporary foundation, it is important to use a shorter stitch length to prevent the stitches from pulling apart or distorting when you remove the paper foundation. With a short stitch length, the paper perforates and is easy to remove at the end of the process. When piecing on a foundation, always place the fabric on the plain side of the foundation with the wrong side of the fabric facing the paper. Then be sure to sew on the printed side of the paper, following the solid line of the pattern.

1. With a fabric glue stick, dab some glue across the area that designates unit 1 (on the unmarked side of the paper).

2. With the wrong side of the fabric facing the plain side of the paper, center the fabric for unit 1, so that it covers the glue-applied area. Make sure that the fabric extends at least ¼" (6 mm) on all sides of the unit 1 area.

3. Flip the foundation over, place the folding template on line 1 (the line between unit 1

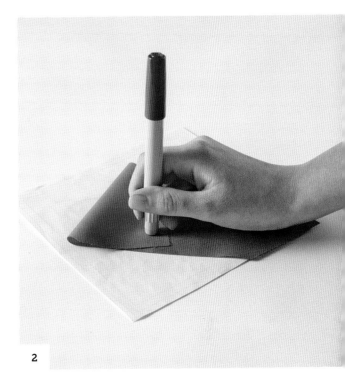

2

and unit 2), and fold the paper back, exposing the excess fabric from unit 1. Folding on the stitch line has the added benefit of making the paper foundation easier to remove at the end of the process.

Consider making a practice block to make sure the scale, color, and value of your fabric choices work well with the block design. Depending on the size of your block, the scale of the fabric pattern can affect the look of the block as well. Smaller-sized blocks look best with fabrics that contain small-scale patterns, or fabrics that read as primarily a solid. Making a practice block also provides an opportunity to verify the stitch length and tension settings of your machine. If the paper is hard to remove from the stitches, increase the stitch length. On the other hand, if the paper perforates completely and falls apart, decrease the stitch length.

(continued)

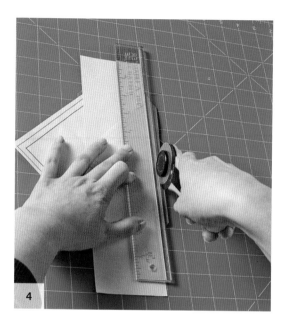

4

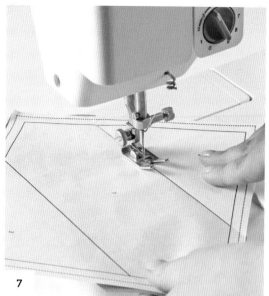

7

4. Place the Add-A-Quarter Ruler over the folded edge with the lip extending ¼" (6 mm).

5. Use the rotary cutter to cut the excess fabric away, leaving a ¼" (6 mm) seam.

6. Remove the folding template, and lay the right side of unit 2 against the right side of unit 1, matching the freshly cut edge of unit 1 with the edge of unit 2 on the joining seam line.

7. Flip the pattern over and hold the fabrics in place (foundation should be face-up with the fabric face-down) and set the foundation pattern and fabrics on the bed of the sewing machine. Use a short stitch length to sew on the line between unit 1 and unit 2 [15–18 stitches per inch (1.4–1.7 mm) for tracing paper or newsprint; 20–22 stitches per inch (1.1–1.3 mm) for copy paper]. Sewing

through the paper and both layers of fabric, sew 2–3 stitches beyond the beginning and end of the line.

8. Clip thread tails close to the stitching.

9. Open fabric 2 and make sure that it covers the foundation shape plus a ¼" (6 mm) seam allowance.

10. With fabric 2 opened, press the seam towards fabric 2 (press from the fabric, not foundation, side). Use cotton setting on the iron, with no steam, as the steam can cause the ink of the pattern to run or make the pattern paper wet, which will distort it.

11. Repeat steps 3 through 10 for each remaining unit in the block. No matter how many pieces a block contains, always use the same process for each unit while constructing the block.

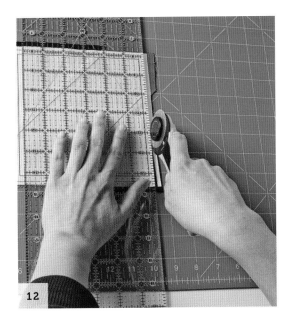

12

shorter stitch length, the paper perforates well and will be easier to remove. While holding the block firmly, tug in opposite directions of the seam line. The paper should snap away from the seam. In blocks with tight, narrow points, it may be necessary to use a pair of tweezers to remove remnants of the paper foundation.

Enlarging/Reducing Patterns

The foundation patterns provided in the book are for 6" (15.24 cm) finished blocks; and the unfinished block is 6½" (16.5 cm). If you want a block in a different size, use the following formula to determine the percentage to enlarge or reduce the pattern on a copy machine:

Block size wanted / Current size of block = Percentage to enlarge or reduce block × 100

To demonstrate, to increase a block from 6" (15.24 cm) to 12" (30.5 cm): $^{12}/_6 = 2 \times 100 = 200\%$

To enlarge the pattern to the desired size, copy it at 200%.

12. Do not worry if the patches extend beyond the edge of the block. After all of the patches are sewn to the foundation, use a rotary cutter and ruler to trim the block along the dotted line with the paper side facing up.

13. 13. Remove the foundation paper from the finished block after trimming. By using a

1 | White House Steps

Skill Level: Beginner

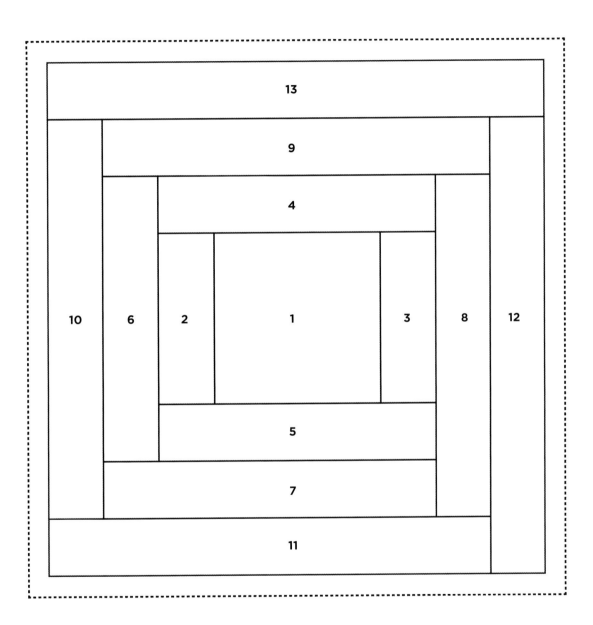

2 | Twisted Log Cabin

Skill Level: Intermediate

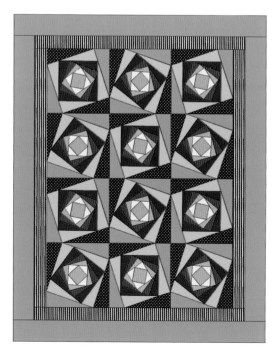

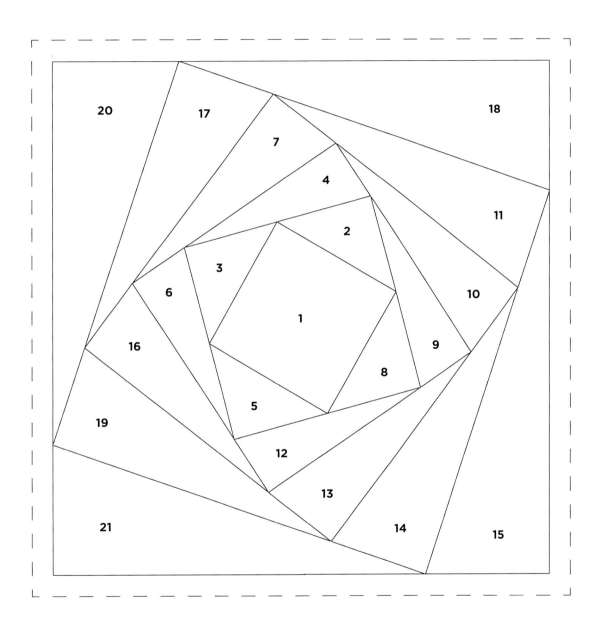

3 | Simple Autograph

Skill Level: Beginner

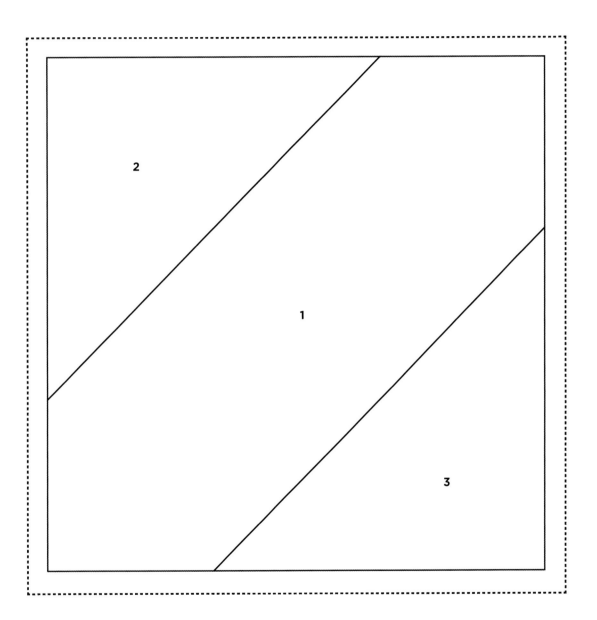

4 | New Jersey

Skill Level: Beginner

Piecing Instructions

1. Foundation-piece the unit. Make 4.

2. Following the piecing diagram, stitch the units together to make the block. Pay attention to the orientation of the block as you sew, as the block is directional.

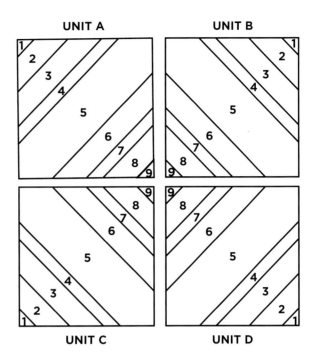

UNIT A UNIT B

UNIT C UNIT D

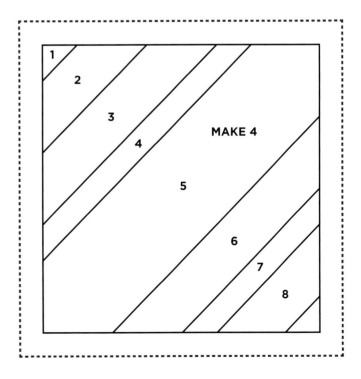

MAKE 4

5 | Little Houses

Skill Level: Beginner

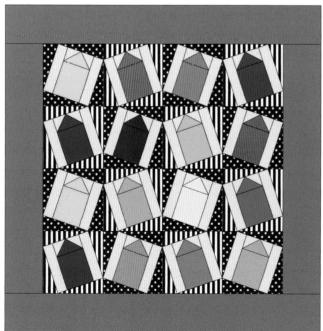

In this quilt layout, half of the blocks use a reverse image of the pattern to emphasize the offset nature of the block.

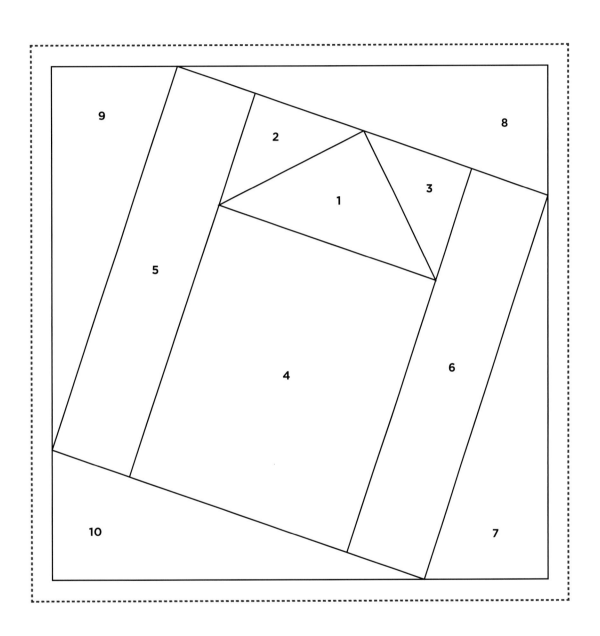

6 | Crazy Quilt

Skill Level: Beginner

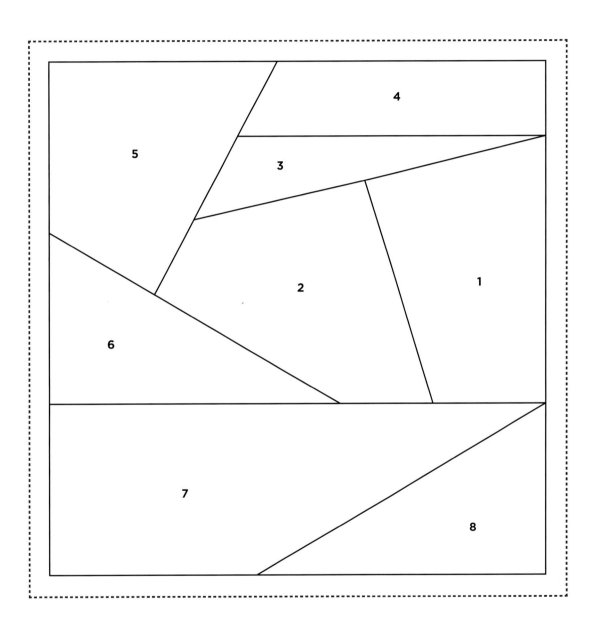

7 | String Quilt

Skill Level: Beginner

Piecing Instructions

1. Stitch the foundation units. Make 4.

2. Stitch the units together to make the block. Pay attention to the orientation of the block as you sew, as the units are directional.

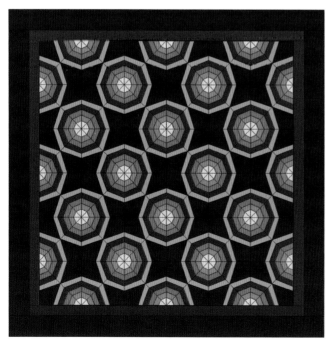

8 | Kaleidoscope

Skill Level: Intermediate

Piecing Instructions

1. Stitch the foundation units. Make 4.

2. Stitch the units together to make the block. Pay attention to the orientation of the block as you sew, as the units are directional.

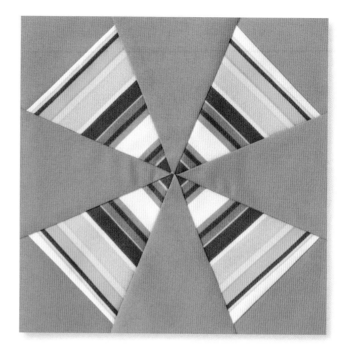

If you use the same fabric for units 1 and 2 in half of the blocks, a secondary circular pattern emerges when you place the blocks together.

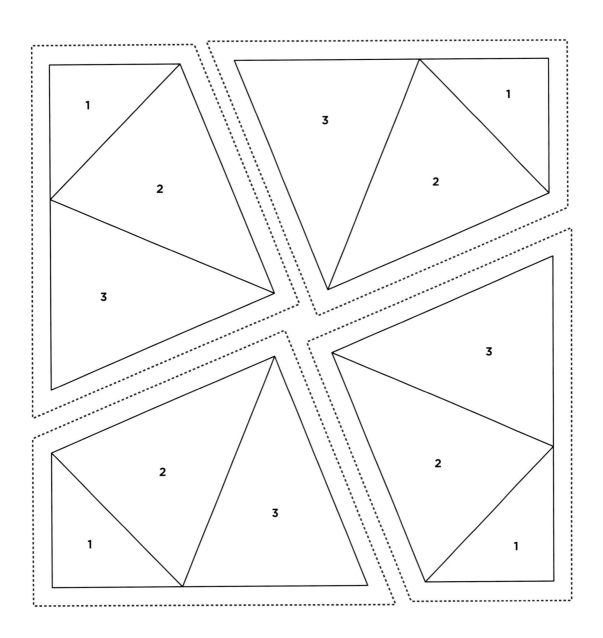

9 | Dakota Star

Skill Level: Intermediate

Piecing Instructions

1. Stitch the foundation units. Make 4.

2. Stitch the units together to make the block. Pay attention to the orientation of the block as you sew, as the units are directional.

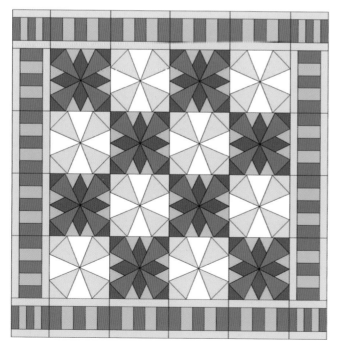

This quilt layout combines two blocks: Kaleidoscope (page 74) and Dakota Star.

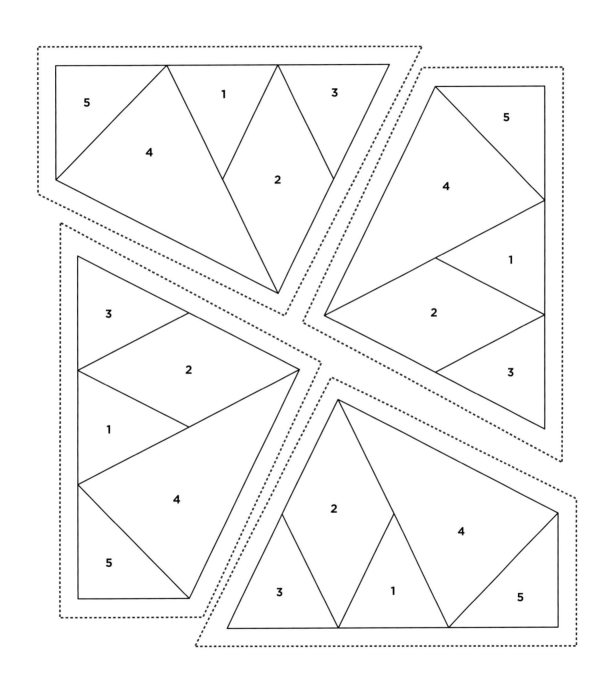

10 | Starry Windmill

Skill Level: Intermediate

Special Cutting Instructions

Cut a 3⅛ (7.9 cm) square for C, or use the template online and cut it precisely.

Piecing Instructions

1. Foundation piece 2 each of unit A and unit B.

2. Stitch a B unit to opposing sides of square C for the center row. Stitch an A unit to opposing sides of the center row to complete the block.

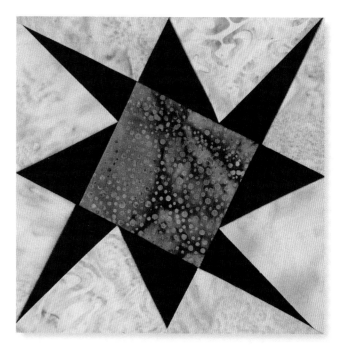

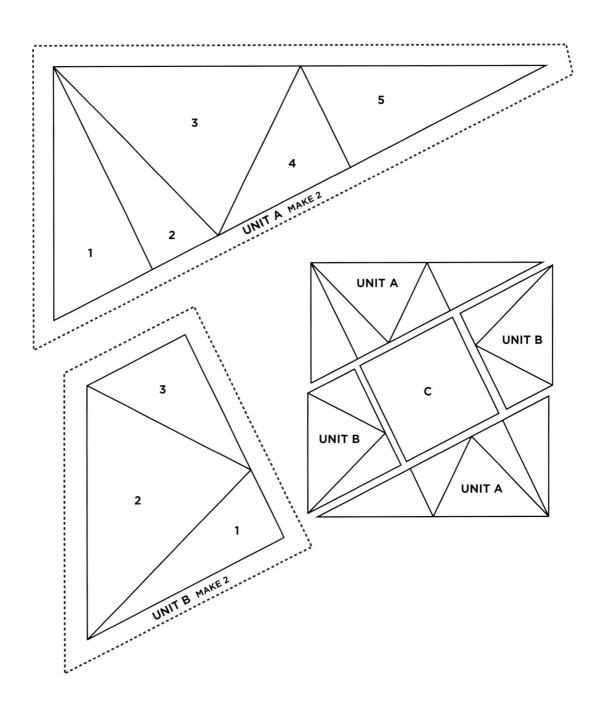

UNIT A MAKE 2

3

4

5

1

2

UNIT B MAKE 2

3

2

1

UNIT A

UNIT B

UNIT B

C

UNIT A

11 | Starry Path

Skill Level: Intermediate

Piecing Instructions

1. Foundation piece four units. Stitch unit A and unit B together to make row 1.

2. Stitch unit C and unit D together to make row 2. Stitch the two rows together to complete the block.

This quilt layout combines two blocks: Starry Path and Starry Windmill (page 78).

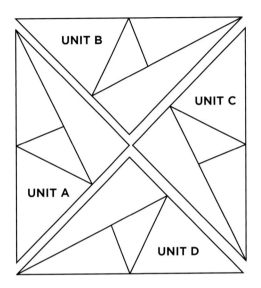

UNIT B

UNIT C

UNIT A

UNIT D

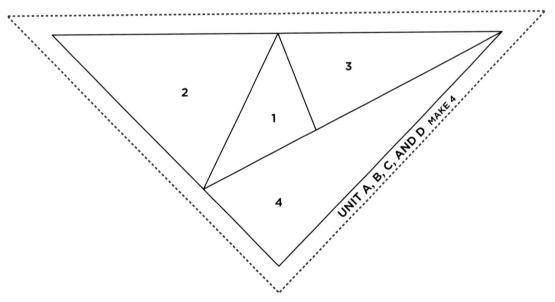

2

3

1

4

UNIT A, B, C, AND D MAKE 4

12 | Wild Goose Chase

Skill Level: Intermediate

Special Cutting Instructions

When cutting the B and D units for this block, cut precisely. Unlike the paper-piecing templates, there is no extra fabric added for seam allowance.

Piecing Instructions

1. **Step 1:** Foundation piece unit A. Make 4.

2. **Step 2:** Stitch a B unit to each side of an A unit to make row 1. Repeat for row 3.

3. **Step 3:** Stitch an A unit to opposing sides of a D unit to make row 2. Stitch the three rows together to complete the block.

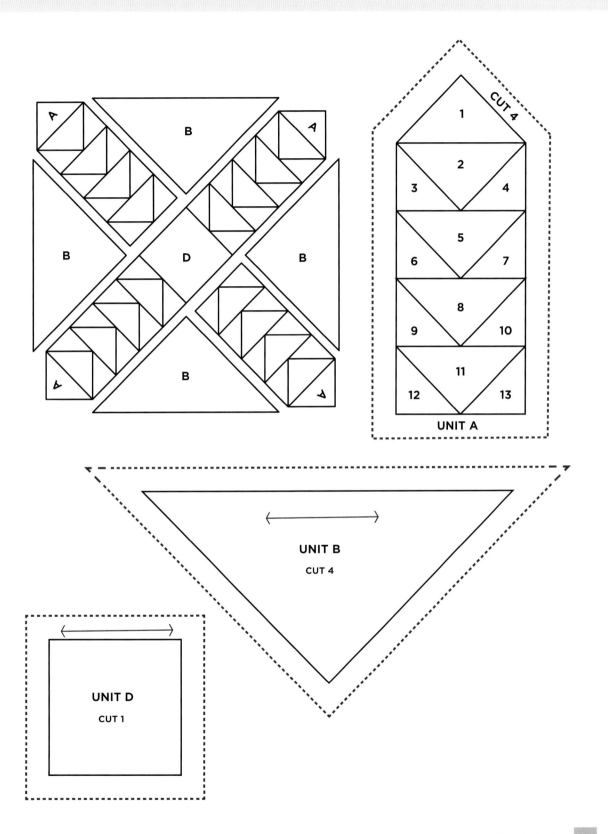

A

B

A

B

D

B

B

A

B

A

CUT 4

1

2

3 4

5

6 7

8

9 10

11

12 13

UNIT A

UNIT B

CUT 4

UNIT D

CUT 1

13 | Chain and Bar

SKILL LEVEL: Intermediate

Piecing Instructions

1. Foundation piece unit A. Make 2.

2. Foundation piece unit B. Make 2.

3. Stitch the two B units together to make a B-B unit.

4. Stitch an A unit to opposing sides of the B-B unit.

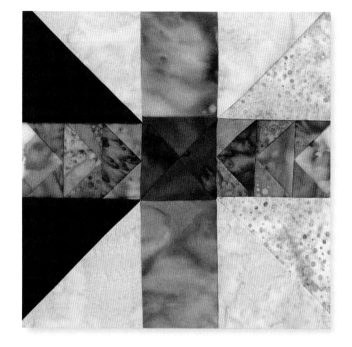

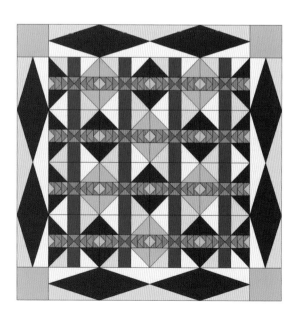

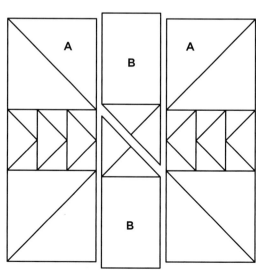

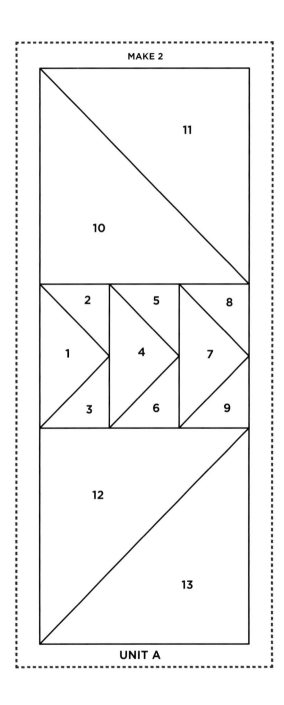

MAKE 2

11

10

2 5 8

1 4 7

3 6 9

12

13

UNIT A

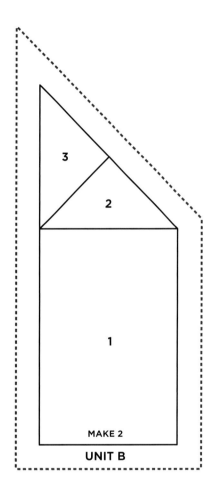

3

2

1

MAKE 2

UNIT B

14 | Pineapple

Skill Level: Intermediate

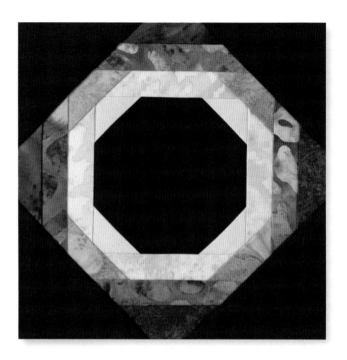

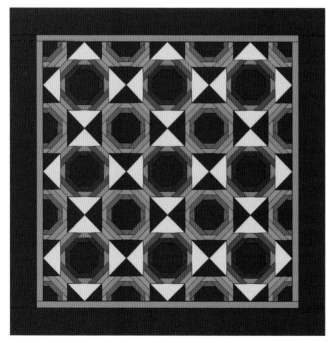

This quilt layout has the blocks on-point.

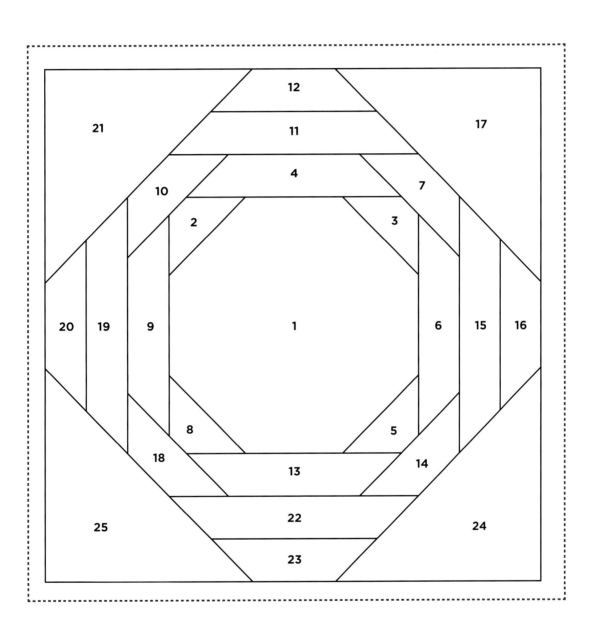

15 | Flying Geese

Skill Level: Intermediate

Piecing Instructions

1. Foundation piece unit A. Make 2.

2. When stitching the two units together to complete the block, reverse the direction of one of the units.

This block is very versatile. Consider using it to create an attractive pieced border.

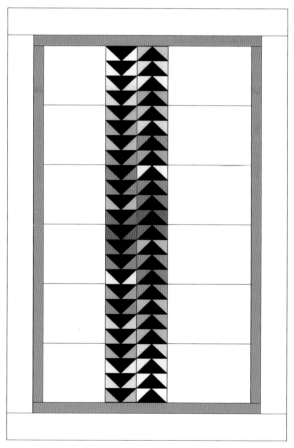

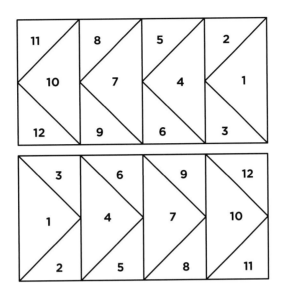

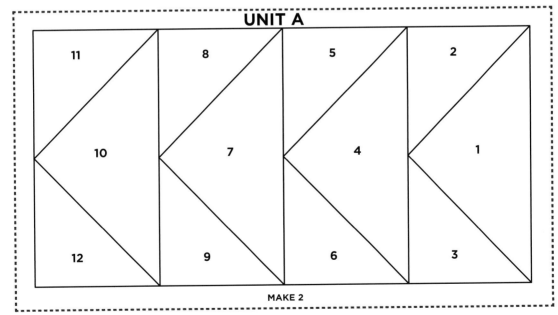

UNIT A

MAKE 2

16 | Stained Glass Surrounded Square

Skill Level: Beginner

This block would also make a good
pieced boarder.

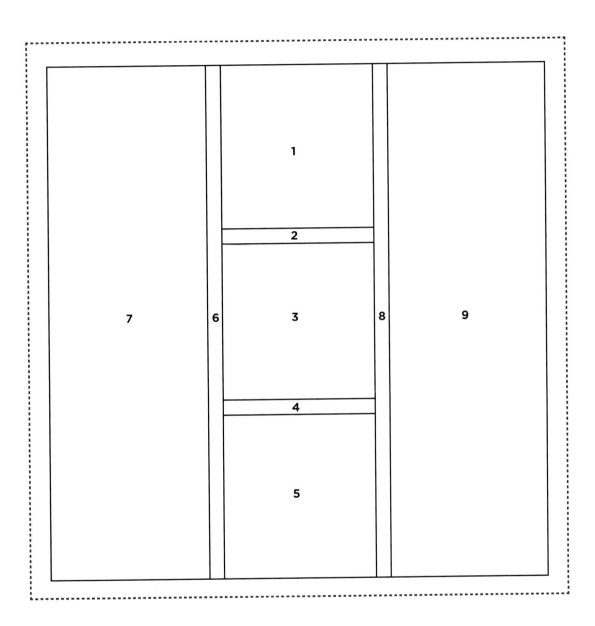

17 | Fan

Skill Level: Advanced

Special Cutting Instructions

When cutting the B unit for this block, it is very important to cut precisely. Unlike the paper piecing templates, no extra fabric has been added to the seam allowance. Cut the units precisely to make it easier to sew the block together.

Piecing Instructions

1. Foundation-piece the fan unit.

2. To stitch the B unit to the foundation-pieced unit, refer to the piecing instructions below.

PIECING INSTRUCTIONS FOR CURVED PIECING

With the right knowledge, curved piecing is easy. The most important tip for success is sewing with an accurate ¼" (6 mm) seam allowance. If sewn with a seam allowance less than ¼" (6 mm), the resulting B unit will be too short, and the A unit too long. Conversely, if sewn with a seam allowance greater than ¼" (6 mm), the B unit will be too long, and the A unit will be too short.

1. Stitch an A unit to a B unit. Stop with the needle down every few stitches and re-align the edges of the fabric. Use a pair of tweezers to feed the fabric edges under the presser foot precisely.

2. To align curves, consider folding the A and B units in half first, and clipping a ⅛" (3 mm) notch in the seam allowance. Put the right sides of units A and B together and pin at the notch.

3. After sewing unit A and unit B together, press toward the convex curve.

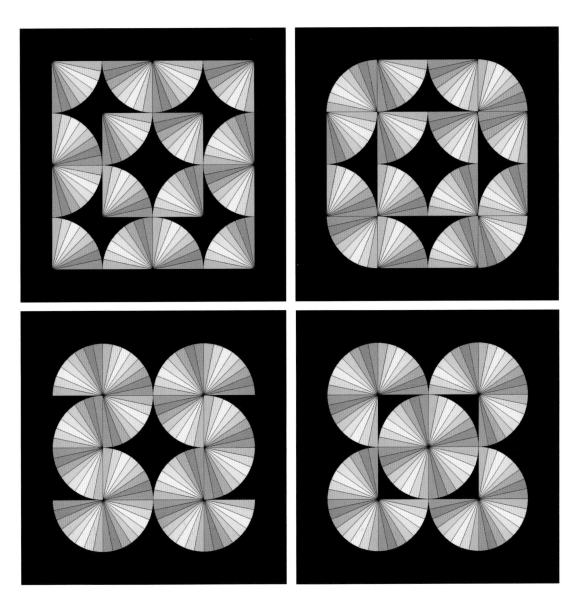

Rotate the blocks before sewing them together until you find a setting that pleases you. Each of these examples uses sixteen fan blocks.

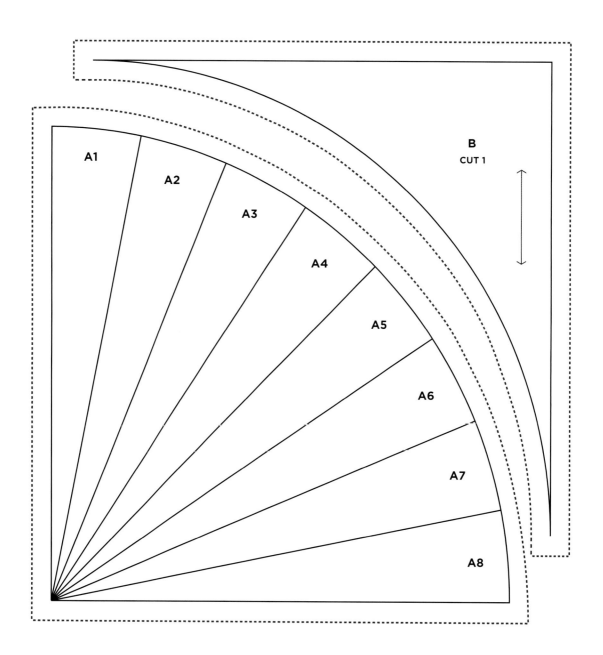

A1

A2

A3

A4

A5

A6

A7

A8

B
CUT 1

Appliqué Blocks

Appliqué involves tracing a shape onto fabric, cutting it out, and stitching it to a background piece of fabric. There are many ways of stitching it down, including raw edge, turned, or reverse appliqué. In raw-edge appliqué, the raw edge of the appliqué remains visible. You may use fusible web to seal the raw edges and prevent fraying. In turned appliqué, you turn the seam underneath the appliqué fabric as you stitch. Finally, in reverse appliqué you stitch a pattern onto two layers of fabric, and then by removing parts of the top layer of fabric, the lower layer of fabric becomes visible. The twenty-five blocks included in this section provide an opportunity to try all three methods. And these appliqué blocks offer a fabulous opportunity to add another layer of visual interest to the quilt by trying out some of the decorative stitches on your machine.

Tools and Supplies

Freezer paper: This product, available in many grocery stores, is useful for accurately cutting appliqué shapes. Trace the appliqué shape onto the dull side of the paper (not the waxy side). With your iron on the cotton setting, iron the waxy side of the paper to the right side of your appliqué fabric. Cut out the shape along the traced line. Remove the freezer paper. Pin or glue baste the appliqué onto the background fabric.

Fusible web: Affix appliqué shapes to the background fabric permanently with a fusible web such as Mistyfuse, Trans-Web by HTC, or Lite Steam-A-Seam 2. These fusibles leave the finished quilt block feeling soft and supple, while other products could leave the fabric feeling too stiff. Follow the manufacturer's directions for these products, as all have slightly different application instructions.

Scissors: When cutting appliqué shapes, be sure to use a sharp scissors that give a crisp cut, free of frayed edges. If cutting small shapes, or sharp angles, a small 4" (10 cm) pair of scissors offers more control. While not required, specialty scissors, such as those sold by Havel, make reverse appliqué easier. Havel's multi-angled scissors have short, curved blades for cutting close to the fabric with blunt tips that won't poke through the fabric.

Pins: Use super-fine silk pins to pin appliqué shapes in place on the background fabric before stitching. They are .50 mm in diameter, with very sharp points. These pins do not distort the fabric nor do they leave unsightly holes. Another pinning option is small ¾" (2 cm) sequin, or appliqué, pins.

Fabric glue: Baste appliqué shapes in place temporarily with a water-soluble glue that dries quickly and does not feel stiff when dry, such as Roxanne Glue-Baste-It, or Sewline fabric glue pen. Look for glue that specifies it is acid-free and/or appropriate for use with fabric. Basting with glue is a great alternative to pins.

Thread: There is a wide variety of threads available for appliqué, depending on the look you want. For mock hand appliqué, try a fine (.004 mm in diameter) invisible monofilament

If the exact shade of thread is unavailable, and the background fabric is light, select a shade lighter than the appliqué fabric. Conversely, if the background fabric is dark, select a shade darker than the appliqué fabric.

thread such as YLI Wonder Invisible Thread. For traditional machine appliqué, use a 50-weight cotton or polyester thread closely matching the appliqué, or a 100-weight thread such as Superior's Kimono Silk Thread or WonderFil Invisafil 100wt Polyester. If the stitching will act as a focal point, select a thread color that contrasts with the appliqué fabric, and use a heavier thread, such as Superior Thread's King Tut.

Tear-away stabilizer: When incorporating satin, zigzag, or decorative stitches with appliqué, use stabilizer underneath the background fabric to support stitch-intensive designs. Using stabilizer avoids unsightly puckering and channels from forming in the fabric. After stitching, reduce bulk by tearing away any excess stabilizer. Be careful not to pull on stitches when removing stabilizer from around (not under) the stitches.

Needles: Match your needle to the thread using the following chart.

Note: When using a small needle, such as 65/9 or 70/10, reduce your sewing speed. These needles are finer than normal sewing machine needles and deflect away from the hook of the bobbin assembly more easily as you change sewing directions. Further, since they are smaller, they are more easily broken.

Needle size—Type	Thread Description	Thread Content (Weight)
65/9 or 70/10—Sharp	Fine	Monofilament .004 mm; Silk 100 weight; Polyester 100 weight
75/11—Embroidery	Medium	Cotton 50 weight; Polyester 50 weight
90/14—Topstitch	Heavy	Cotton 40 weight; Polyester 40 weight

General Techniques

There are two basic ways to prepare appliqué shapes: raw edge and turned.

Raw-Edge Appliqué

To do raw-edge appliqué, trace the actual size shape (with no seam allowance) directly onto the wrong side of the fabric. If the design is directional, be sure to reverse the image before tracing, since the image is marked on the wrong side of the fabric. The easiest method for tracing the design onto fabric is to use freezer paper, fusible web, and a light box.

For freezer paper

1. Trace the pattern onto the non-wax side of the freezer paper (a light box simplifies this task).

2. Roughly cut out the shape from the freezer paper outside the drawn line.

3. Iron the waxy side of the freezer paper to the right side of the appliqué fabric.

4. Using sharp scissors, cut out the appliqué shape along the marked line. Take care when cutting to avoid fraying the edges of the fabric.

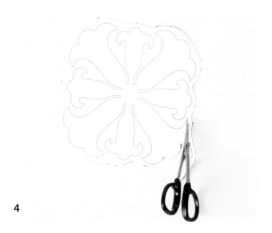

4

5. Pin or glue-baste the appliqué shape in place on the background fabric. Stitch the appliqué shape to the background fabric with the desired stitch (straight, zigzag, satin, or decorative).

For fusible web

1. Trace the pattern onto the paper side of a lightweight fusible web, such as Lite Steam-A-Seam 2.

2. Roughly cut out each shape from the fusible web, but do not cut on the marked line.

3. Following the manufacturer's instructions, fuse the adhesive to the wrong side of the appliqué fabric.

4. Using sharp scissors, cut out the appliqué shape along the marked line. Take care when cutting to avoid fraying the edges of the fabric.

5. Remove the paper from the back of the cut appliqué shape, leaving a fine layer of adhesive on the back of fabric.

6. Following the manufacturer's directions, use the appropriate settings on your iron to fuse the appliqué in place on the background fabric.

7. Stitch the appliqué shape to the background fabric with the desired stitch (straight, zigzag, satin, or decorative).

Turned Appliqué

Like the finished look of needle-turned appliqué, but hate the laborious nature of hand stitching? Try this technique for mock hand appliqué look using the blind-hem stitch on your machine.

1. Trace the appliqué shape onto sew-in interfacing (for use with sheer to light fabrics). Do not include a seam allowance in the traced shape; trace the shape in the finished size. Leave enough space between each traced shape for a seam allowance of ½" (12 mm) or more.

2. Layer the interfacing on top of the appliqué fabric, with the right side of the fabric up. Pin the interfacing and appliqué fabric together to prevent shifting.

3. Stitch on the marked line, all the way around the shape, leaving no gaps. Use either a regular straight stitch with the feed dogs up, or free motion stitching with the feed dogs down. If you are comfortable with free motion sewing, it is an easier way to handle tight corners and small details.

4. Trim around the appliqué shape with a scant ¼" to ⅛" (6 to 3 mm) seam allowance.

5. Clip the seam allowance at corners and curves.

6. Clip a slit in the interfacing *only.* Take care not to cut into the appliqué fabric. The slit is just large enough to turn the fabric through the slit; do not cut the slit all the way to the edge of the appliqué shape. By turning the fabric inside-out through the slit, the raw edges disappear.

7. Turn the appliqué shape right-side out through the slit in the interfacing.

8. Use a bone folder or chopstick to smooth the seams and corners.

9. Press with a warm iron for synthetic fabric (not cotton) since most interfacings are made of polyester. Too hot of an iron may melt polyester interfacing. Stitch the appliqué shape to the background fabric with the desired stitch (straight, zigzag, satin, or decorative).

1

4

6

8

Stitching Methods

There are several stitch choices for doing appliqué with a sewing machine: straight, zigzag, satin, decorative, and blind hem (mock hand appliqué). Each gives a different effect, and their use is a matter of personal preference. All of them use an open-toe embroidery foot, which provides better visibility. The ability to see the edge of the appliqué is important as you stitch. Traditionally, the thread color matches the appliqué (although you have permission to break this rule). Machine embroidery thread, either cotton or polyester, is the best choice, since it is thinner than regular cotton thread. Another choice is nylon monofilament thread, which requires adjusting the upper thread tension to a lower setting. In the bobbin, use a neutral or matching color bobbin thread. It is a good habit to do small sample to test the tension setting, and see if any adjustments are necessary. In machine appliqué, good thread tension does not show any bobbin thread on the top. If the bobbin thread is visible on the top of the fabric, loosen the top tension or tighten the bobbin tension.

Some machines have a needle down feature, which stops sewing with the needle in the down position. If your machine has this feature, use it; it saves time and gives a more professional result. In addition, if your machine came with a free-hand knee lift bar that raises and lowers the presser foot, use it as well. It allows you to keep your hands on the fabric to pivot while you raise and lower the presser foot hands free, which increases productivity, and effectively gives you a "third hand" while sewing.

Straight Stitch

In this method, stitch the appliqué fabric onto the background fabric with a straight machine stitch. An open-toe embroidery foot will work for this method, but you may find an edge stitch foot even easier. The open-toe embroidery foot has great visibility, while the edge-stitch foot has a guide to help stitch straight along an edge. Try them both to see which you prefer.

1. Pin or glue the shape in place. If using pins, silk or appliqué pins are better than sewing pins because they are thin and have very sharp points. If using glue, make sure it is fabric-safe and water-soluble.

2. Start stitching on a curve or straight edge, rather than an inner or outer point, as it is easier to hide your starts and stops.

3. Select the straight stitch on your sewing machine, and alter the stitch length to around fifteen stitches per inch (1.7 mm). To anchor your stitches at the beginning, lower the feed dogs, and take around four stitches in place. Raise the feed dogs, and begin stitching. Stitch from $\frac{1}{16}$" to $\frac{1}{8}$" (1.5 mm to 3 mm) from the edge of the appliqué shape.

4. If your sewing machine has a needle down feature, use it. To stitch inner and outer points, stop with the needle down, pivot the fabric, and resume stitching.

5. To finish sewing, drop the feed dogs of your machine, and take four stitches in place. This eliminates the need to backstitch or overlap stitching, which is unsightly.

Zigzag or Satin Stitch

In this method, a zigzag or satin stitch covers the raw edge of the appliqué shape. Use a layer of tear-away stabilizer underneath the quilt block to support stitch-intensive designs. Begin by testing the desired stitch width (SW) and stitch length (SL) on some fabric scraps. For a sparser zigzag stitch, use a stitch width of 2.0 mm, and a stitch length of .7 mm. For a traditional satin stitch, the stitch is denser, with a stitch width of 3.0 mm and a stitch length of .3 mm. On a scrap of fabric try varying settings to see which stitch length and stitch width is desirable.

Repeat steps 1–4 for straight stitch appliqué, substituting a zigzag stitch. To pivot on curves, keep the needle on the outside edge for outer curves, and keep the needle on the inside edge for inner curves. Further, when rounding a curve, stop and pivot with the needle in the down position every few stitches. To satin stitch around inner points, stitch slightly beyond the inner point, pivot, and stitch down the previous stitches, overlapping the previous stitches.

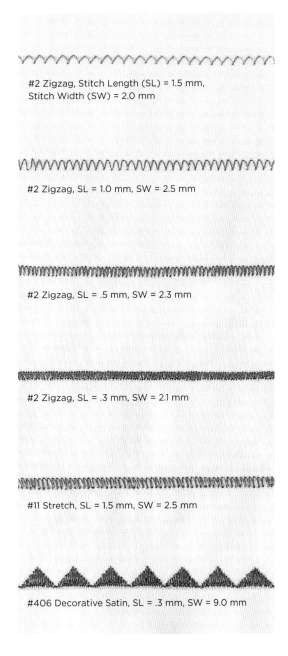

#2 Zigzag, Stitch Length (SL) = 1.5 mm, Stitch Width (SW) = 2.0 mm

#2 Zigzag, SL = 1.0 mm, SW = 2.5 mm

#2 Zigzag, SL = .5 mm, SW = 2.3 mm

#2 Zigzag, SL = .3 mm, SW = 2.1 mm

#11 Stretch, SL = 1.5 mm, SW = 2.5 mm

#406 Decorative Satin, SL = .3 mm, SW = 9.0 mm

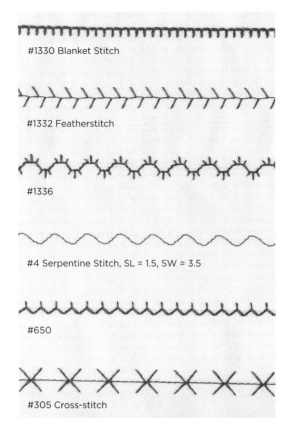

#1330 Blanket Stitch

#1332 Featherstitch

#1336

#4 Serpentine Stitch, SL = 1.5, SW = 3.5

#650

#305 Cross-stitch

Zigzag/Satin Stitch Sampler

Decorative Stitch

For this method, a decorative stitch covers the raw edge of the appliqué shape. Use a layer of tear-away stabilizer underneath the quilt block to support stitch-intensive designs. Begin by testing the desired stitch width and stitch length on some fabric scraps. Most machines have a wide variety of decorative stitches suited for this task.

The most popular choice is a blanket stitch, which takes one stitch forward, swings to the left and takes a stitch, and then swings to the right and takes a stitch (hitting the same hole twice).

Repeat steps 1–4 for straight stitch appliqué, substituting the preferred decorative stitch.

Mock Hand Appliqué

For this method, a blind hemstitch with invisible monofilament thread gives a look closely matching the effect of hand appliqué.

Needle: Use a small needle (60/8 or 70/10), since it leaves a smaller hole and provides more control over tension. Reduce sewing speed when using these small needles, as they are more fragile and break easier.

Thread: Use the clear monofilament on light fabrics, and the smoke-colored monofilament on dark fabrics. Some brands of monofilament thread are too thick and stiff. These coarser monofilament threads will not provide the "hand-sewn" look. A monofilament thread with a fine diameter (.004 mm) and a soft, smooth texture (rather than wiry), is desired.

Stitch Settings and Tension: The blind-hem stitch on your machine takes 4–7 straight stitches to the right, and then zigzags to the left. The straight stitches are on the background fabric, and the zigzag stitch takes a small bite into the appliqué fabric. Test the stitch width, stitch length, and tension on a scrap piece of fabric before stitching on your block. These stitches are small (and ripping them out is no fun), so practice the stitch on a sample before stitching on a final project.

• Adjust the stitch length and width to around 25 stitches per inch (.6 mm to 1 mm). The zigzag stitches should just catch two to three threads of the appliqué fabric.

• The extremely short stitch length calls for reducing the upper tension of the machine to a setting such as 2.0.

• If your bobbin case has a pigtail or finger, thread the bobbin thread through this, as doing so will automatically increase the bobbin tension and pull the top thread to the back side of the fabric.

Repeat steps 1–4 for straight stitch appliqué (page 100), substituting a blind-hem stitch. Insert the needle into the background fabric, right along the edge of the appliqué fabric. The straight stitches should nestle into the background fabric next to the appliqué shape, and their small size, coupled with the monofilament thread, makes them disappear. When the needle swings to the left, the zigzag portion of the blind hemstitch just catches the edge of the appliqué, giving the effect of a hand stitch.

If you have to press your appliqué block after stitching, use an iron on a synthetic or wool setting to avoid melting the monofilament thread.

To place the appliqué shapes on the background fabric, trace the master pattern onto clear vinyl. Tape the vinyl on the top edge of the background fabric. Use this vinyl overlay as a guide when you place the appliqué shapes. Place the appliqué shapes underneath the vinyl on the background fabric, moving them into position. Once properly placing the shapes, remove the vinyl, and continue with the appliqué process. This method is applicable to both turned and fused appliqué.

Default Blind Hem Stitch, SL = 1.5 mm, SW = 2.0 mm

Mock Hand Appliqué Blind Hem Stitch, SL = .6 mm, SW = 1.0 mm

The appliqué patterns provided in the book are for 6" (15.25 cm) finished blocks; the unfinished block is 6½" (16.5 cm). If you want a block in a different size, use the following formula to determine the percentage to enlarge or reduce the pattern on a copy machine:

Block size wanted / Current size of block = Percentage to enlarge or reduce block × 100

For example, to increase a block from 6" to 10" (15.25 cm to 25.5 cm), do the following: 10 ÷ 6 = 1.67 × 100 = 167%

To enlarge the pattern the desired size, copy it at 167%.

1 | Golden Wedding Ring

Skill Level: Beginner

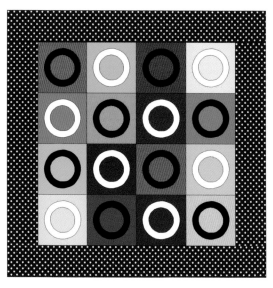

Appliqué Instructions for a 6-Inch Finished Block

1. Trace the pattern onto the right side of a 6½" (16.5 cm) piece of fabric. Layer that fabric on top of a contrasting fabric, right sides up, with a piece of tear-away stabilizer underneath the fabric sandwich. Pin or glue-baste them together to prevent shifting.

2. Thread your machine with a fine- to medium-weight thread that matches the top fabric. Straight stitch on the marked lines with 13 stitches per inch (or 2.0 mm).

3. Carefully cut away the top fabric from the circle ring (B on the pattern). Trim as close to the stitching line as possible, without cutting the stitches.

4. Using a decorative stitch on your machine, stitch over the raw edge of the fabric and the previous stitching.

5. Tear away any excess stabilizer from the back of the block, taking care not to pull on stitches.

6. Trim excess B fabric away from the back of the block, leaving a generous ¼" (6 mm) seam allowance.

3

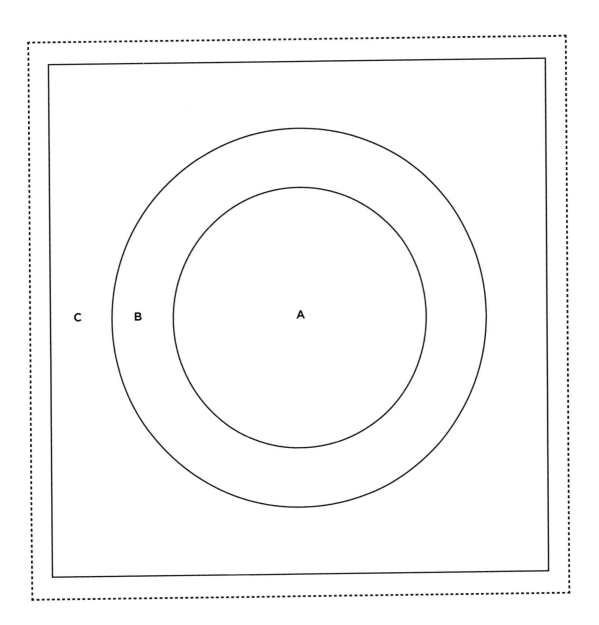

2 | Quarter Turn

Skill Level: Beginner

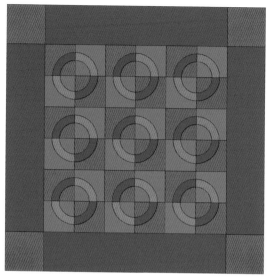

Piecing Diagram

Appliqué Instructions for a 6-Inch Finished Block

1. Trace the pattern onto the right side of two 7" (17.75 cm) pieces of fabric. The fabrics should contrast with each other, as the construction of this block involves making two blocks at once, cutting the block into fourths, and then swapping half of the units between the two blocks.

2. Follow the instructions for the Golden Wedding Ring block (page 104) for each of the two blocks required for this pair of Quarter Turn blocks.

3. Cut each block into fourths (refer to piecing diagram).

4. Swap units B and C between the two blocks to create contrasting quadrants.

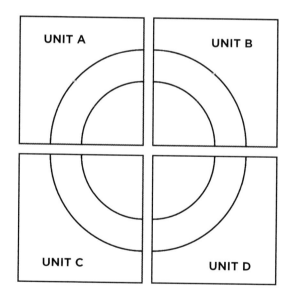

5. Stitch units A and B into row one; stitch units C and D into row two. Join row one and row two. Repeat for both blocks.

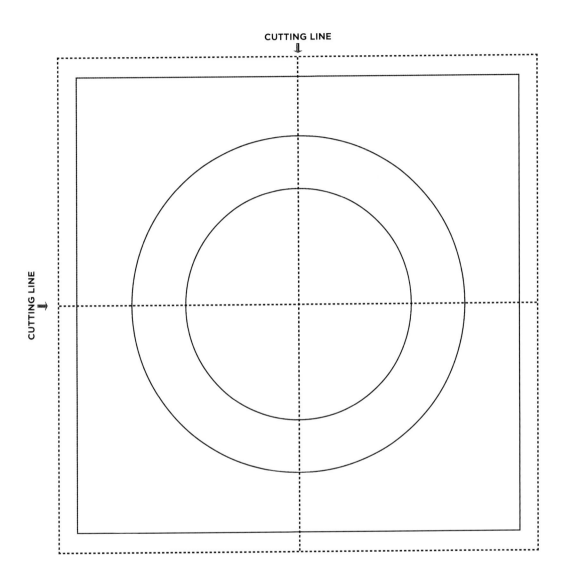

CUTTING LINE

CUTTING LINE

3 | Gears

Skill Level: Beginner

Appliqué Pattern

1. Trace the pattern onto a lightweight fusible web, such as Steam-A-Seam 2. Roughly cut out each shape from the fusible web, but do not cut on the marked line.

2. Following the manufacturer's instructions, fuse the adhesive to the wrong side of the appliqué fabrics. Use a sharp scissors to cut out the appliqué shapes on the marked line. Take care when cutting to avoid fraying the edges of the fabric.

3. Remove the paper from the back of the cut appliqué shapes, leaving a fine layer of adhesive on the back of fabric.

4. Cut a 6½" (16.5 cm) piece of background fabric. Position the background fabric under the master pattern (page 103). Position the appliqués in place on the background fabric.

5. Following the manufacturer's instructions, fuse the appliqué shapes to the background fabric.

6. Stitch the appliqué shapes to the background fabric, using the desired decorative stitch.

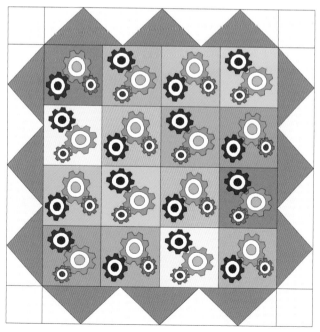

4 | Hex Sign

Skill Level: Intermediate

Appliqué Pattern

1. Trace the four patterns onto a lightweight fusible web, such as Steam-A-Seam 2. Roughly cut out each shape from the fusible web, but do not cut on the marked line.

2. Following the manufacturer's instructions, fuse the adhesive to the wrong side of the appliqué fabrics. Use a sharp scissors to cut out the appliqué shapes on the marked line. Take care when cutting to avoid fraying the edges of the fabric.

3. Remove the paper from the back of the cut appliqué shapes, leaving a fine layer of adhesive on the back of fabric.

4. Cut a 6½" (16.5 cm) piece of background fabric. Position the background fabric under the master pattern (page 103). Position the appliqués in place on the background fabric, adding them in numbered order.

5. Following the manufacturer's instructions, fuse the appliqué shapes to the background fabric and each other.

6. Stitch the appliqué shapes to the background fabric, using the desired decorative stitch.

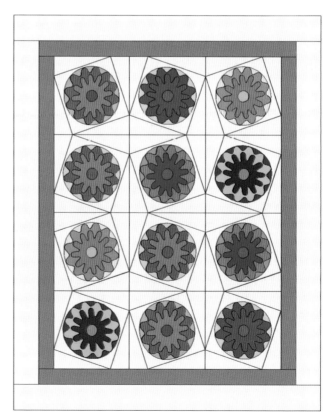

5 | Oak Leaf

Skill Level: Beginner

Appliqué Pattern

1. Trace the pattern onto a lightweight fusible web, such as Steam-A-Seam 2. Roughly cut out the shape from the fusible web, but do not cut on the marked line.

2. Following the manufacturer's instructions, fuse the adhesive to the wrong side of the appliqué fabric. Use a sharp scissors to cut out the appliqué shape on the marked line. Take care when cutting to avoid fraying the edges of the fabric.

3. Remove the paper from the back of the cut appliqué shape, leaving a fine layer of adhesive on the back of fabric.

4. Cut a 6½" (16.5 cm) piece of background fabric. Position the background fabric under the master pattern (page 103). Position the appliqué in place on the background fabric.

5. Following the manufacturer's instructions, fuse the appliqué shape to the background fabric.

6. Stitch the appliqué shape to the background fabric, using the desired decorative stitch.

6 | Jacks

Skill Level: Beginner

1. Trace the pattern onto a lightweight fusible web, such as Steam-A-Seam 2. Roughly cut out the shape from the fusible web, but do not cut on the marked line.

2. Following the manufacturer's instructions, fuse the adhesive to the wrong side of the appliqué fabric. Use a sharp scissors to cut out the appliqué shape on the marked line. Take care when cutting to avoid fraying the edges of the fabric.

3. Remove the paper from the back of the cut appliqué shape, leaving a fine layer of adhesive on the back of fabric.

4. Cut a 6½" (16.5 cm) piece of background fabric. Position the background fabric under the master pattern (page 103). Position the appliqué in place on the background fabric.

5. Following the manufacturer's instructions, fuse the appliqué shape to the background fabric.

6. Stitch the appliqué shape to the background fabric, using the desired decorative stitch.

7 | Mod Diamond

Skill Level: Beginner

Appliqué Pattern

1. Trace the pattern onto a lightweight fusible web, such as Steam-A-Seam 2. Roughly cut out each shape from the fusible web, but do not cut on the marked line.

2. Following the manufacturer's instructions, fuse the adhesive to the wrong side of the appliqué fabric. Use a sharp scissors to cut out the appliqué shape on the marked line. Take care when cutting to avoid fraying the edges of the fabric.

3. Remove the paper from the back of the cut appliqué shape, leaving a fine layer of adhesive on the back of fabric.

4. Cut a 6½" (16.5 cm) piece of background fabric. Position the background fabric under the master pattern (page 103). Position the appliqué in place on the background fabric.

5. Following the manufacturer's instructions, fuse the appliqué shape to the background fabric.

6. Stitch the appliqué shape to the background fabric using the desired decorative stitch.

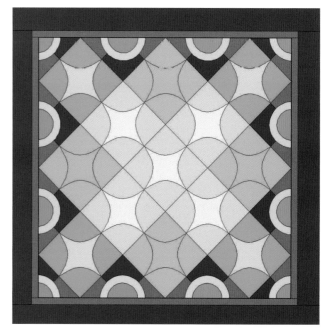

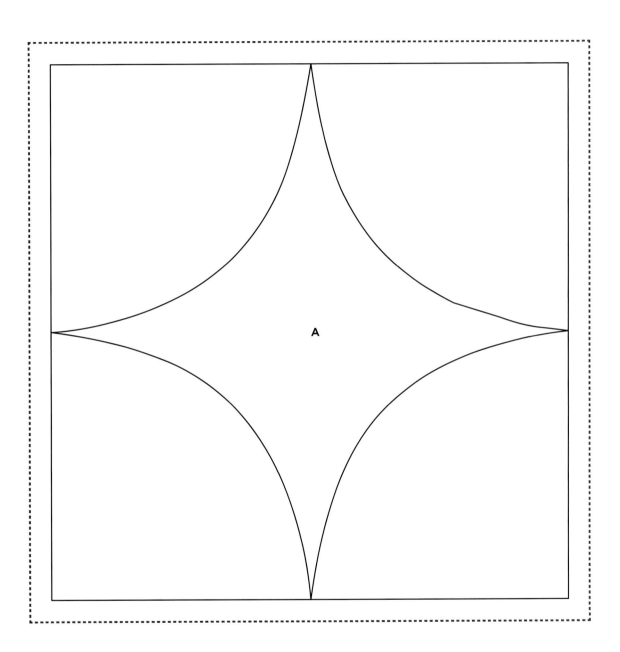

A

8 | Celtic Knot

Skill Level: Beginner

1. Trace the pattern onto a lightweight fusible web, such as Steam-A-Seam 2. Roughly cut out each shape from the fusible web, but do not cut on the marked line.

2. Following the manufacturer's instructions, fuse the adhesive to the wrong side of the appliqué fabrics. Use a sharp scissors to cut out the appliqué shapes on the marked line. Take care when cutting to avoid fraying the edges of the fabric.

3. Remove the paper from the back of the cut appliqué shapes, leaving a fine layer of adhesive on the back of fabric.

4. Cut a 6½" (16.5 cm) piece of background fabric. Position the background fabric under the master pattern (page 103). Position the appliqués in place on the background fabric.

5. Following the manufacturer's instructions, fuse the appliqué shapes to the background fabric.

6. Stitch the appliqué shapes to the background fabric, using the desired decorative stitch.

9 | Posy

Skill Level: Beginner

1. Trace the appliqué pattern onto a lightweight fusible web, such as Steam-A-Seam 2. Roughly cut out each shape from the fusible web, but do not cut on the marked line.

2. Following the manufacturer's instructions, fuse the adhesive to the wrong side of the appliqué fabric. Use a sharp scissors to cut out the appliqué shapes on the marked lines. Take care when cutting to avoid fraying the edges of the fabric.

3. Remove the paper from the back of the cut appliqué shapes, leaving a fine layer of adhesive on the back of fabric.

4. Cut a 6½" (16.5 cm) piece of background fabric. Position the background fabric under the master pattern (page 103). Position the appliqués in place on the background fabric, ending with the circle.

5. Following the manufacturer's instructions, fuse the appliqué shapes to the background fabric. Take care to layer the stem of the posy underneath the circle.

6. Stitch the appliqué shapes to the background fabric, using the desired decorative stitch.

10 | Fantasy Flower

Skill Level: Beginner

1. Trace the appliqué pattern onto a lightweight fusible web, such as Steam-A-Seam 2. Roughly cut out each shape from the fusible web, but do not cut on the marked line.

2. Following the manufacturer's instructions, fuse the adhesive to the wrong side of the appliqué fabric. Use a sharp scissors to cut out the appliqué shapes on the marked lines. Take care when cutting to avoid fraying the edges of the fabric.

3. Remove the paper from the back of the cut appliqué shapes, leaving a fine layer of adhesive on the back of fabric.

4. Cut a 6½" (16.5 cm) piece of background fabric. Position the background fabric under the master pattern (page 103). Position the appliqués in place on the background fabric, ending with the circle.

5. Following the manufacturer's instructions, fuse the appliqué shapes to the background fabric. Take care to layer the stem of the posy underneath the circle.

6. Stitch the appliqué shapes to the background fabric, using the desired decorative stitch.

This quilt layout combines three blocks. The interior of the quilt includes the following blocks: Posy (page 120), and Mod Diamond (page 116). The border of the quilt is Fantasy Flower blocks.

11 | Tulip

Skill Level: Beginner

1. Trace the five appliqué patterns onto a lightweight fusible web, such as Steam-A-Seam 2. Roughly cut out each shape from the fusible web, but do not cut on the marked line.

2. Following the manufacturer's instructions, fuse the adhesive to the wrong side of the appliqué fabrics. Use a sharp scissors to cut out the appliqué shapes on the marked lines. Take care when cutting to avoid fraying the edges of the fabric.

3. Remove the paper from the back of the cut appliqué shapes, leaving a fine layer of adhesive on the back of fabric.

4. Cut a 6½" (16.5 cm) piece of background fabric. Position the background fabric under the master pattern (page 103). Position the appliqués in place on the background fabric in numbered order.

5. Following the manufacturer's instructions, fuse the appliqué shapes to the background fabric. Take care to layer the stem of the flower underneath the flower and the center petal over the side petals.

6. Stitch the appliqué shapes to the background fabric using the desired decorative stitch.

This quilt layout combines two blocks: Dresden Flower Fan (page 126) and Tulip.

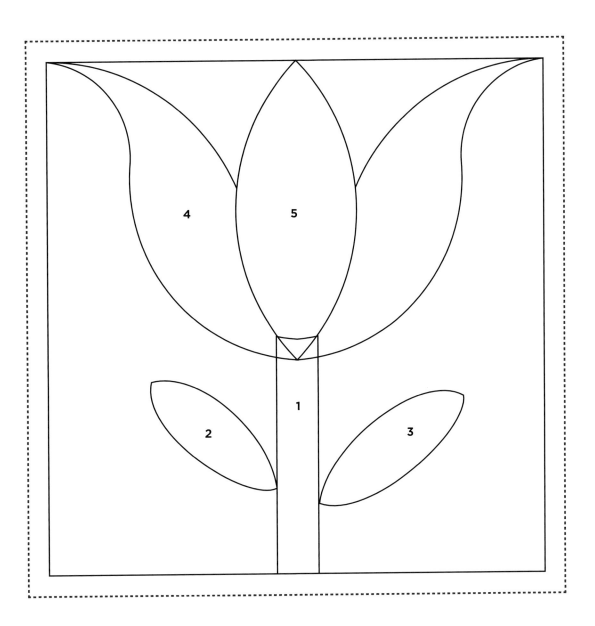

12 | Dresden Flower Fan

Skill Level: Intermediate

1. Using the provided template, cut 5 flower petals.

2. Fold the petals in half lengthwise, with the right sides together.

3. Stitch the top edge of each petal with a ¼" (6 mm) seam.

4. Turn the top edge right-side out and press.

5. Place two petals with right sides facing and stitch the long sides together with a ¼-inch seam. Continue adding petals, one at a time, until all five petals are stitched together. Press the seams in one direction.

6. Appliqué the flower unit created in the previous step to a 6½" (16.5 cm) piece of background fabric; use a decorative stitch of your choosing.

7. To reduce bulk, cut away any excess background fabric underneath the Dresden flower unit. Cut approximately ½" (12 mm) from the decorative stitching line.

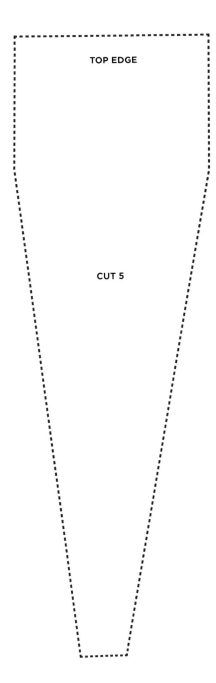

TOP EDGE

CUT 5

13 | Dresden Plate

Skill Level: Intermediate

1. Using the provided template, cut eight fan blade units.

2. Fold the fan blade units in half lengthwise with the right sides of together and stitch the top edge of each unit using a ¼" (6 mm) seam.

3. Turn the top edge of each fan blade unit right-side out and press.

4. Place two fan blade units with right sides facing and stitch the long sides together using a ¼" (6 mm) seam. Continue adding fan blade units, one at a time, until all eight units are stitched together. Press the seams in one direction.

5. Using the provided template, cut one pie-shaped wedge. Sew the pie-shaped wedge to the unit created in the previous step with a ¼" (6 mm) seam. (For more information on curved piecing, refer to the instructions on page 92.) Press toward the pie-shaped wedge.

6. Appliqué the unit created in the previous step to a 6½" (16.5 cm) piece of background fabric, using a decorative stitch of your choosing.

7. To reduce bulk, cut away any excess background fabric from underneath the Dresden Plate unit; cut approximately ½" (12 mm) from the decorative stitching line.

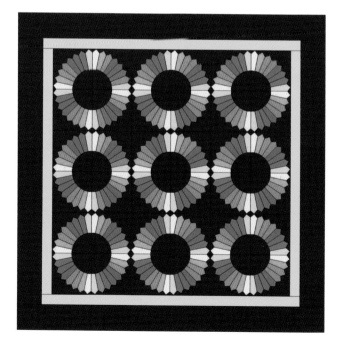

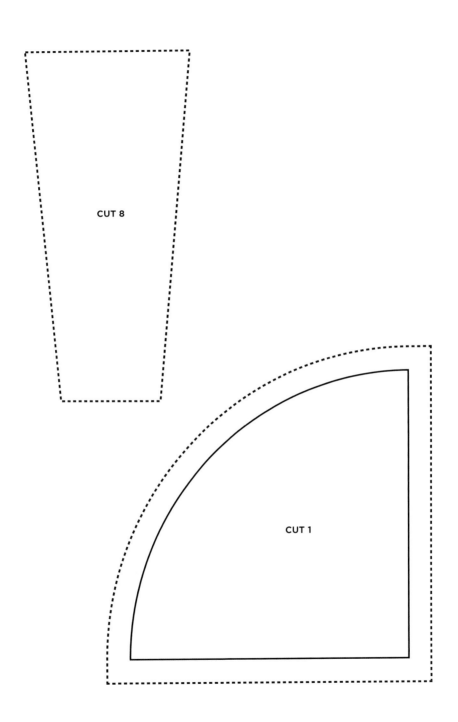

CUT 8

CUT 1

14 | Scalloped Swag

Skill Level: Beginner

1. Trace the appliqué patterns onto a lightweight fusible web, such as Steam-A-Seam 2. Roughly cut out each shape from the fusible web, but do not cut on the marked line.

2. Following the manufacturer's instructions, fuse the adhesive to the wrong side of the appliqué fabrics. Use a sharp scissors to cut out the appliqué shapes on the marked lines. Take care when cutting to avoid fraying the edges of the fabric.

3. Remove the paper from the back of the cut appliqué shapes, leaving a fine layer of adhesive on the back of fabric.

4. Cut a 6½" (16.5 cm) piece of background fabric. Position the background fabric under the master pattern (page 103). Position the appliqués in place on the background fabric in numbered order.

5. Following the manufacturer's instructions, fuse the appliqué shapes to the background fabric. Take care to layer 1 underneath 2.

6. Stitch the appliqué shapes to the background fabric, using the desired decorative stitch.

This quilt layout combines three blocks. The interior of the quilt includes the following blocks: Posy (page 120), and Mod Diamond (page 116). The border of the quilt is Scalloped Swag blocks.

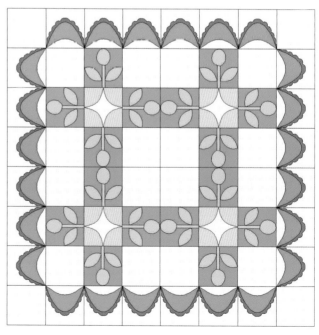

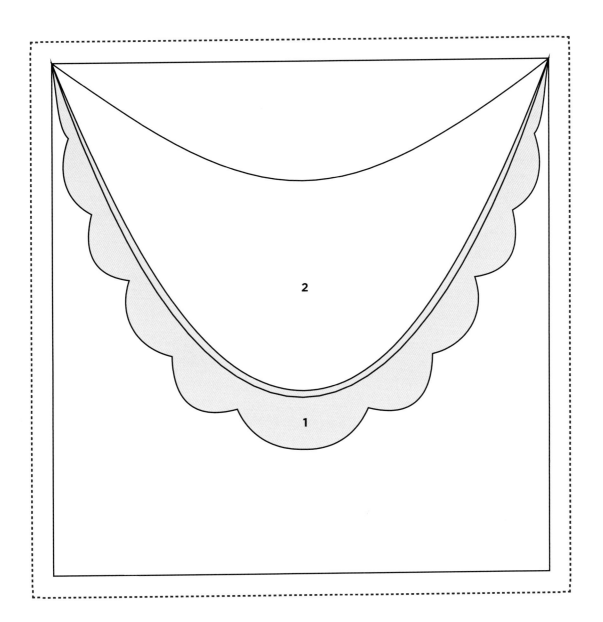

15 | Spikey Flower Swag

Skill Level: Intermediate

1. Trace the appliqué patterns onto a lightweight fusible web, such as Steam-A-Seam 2. Roughly cut out each shape from the fusible web, but do not cut on the marked line.

2. Following the manufacturer's instructions, fuse the adhesive to the wrong side of the appliqué fabrics. Use a sharp scissors to cut out the appliqué shapes on the marked lines. Take care when cutting to avoid fraying the edges of the fabric.

3. Remove the paper from the back of the cut appliqué shapes, leaving a fine layer of adhesive on the back of fabric.

4. Cut a 6½" (16.5 cm) piece of background fabric. Position the background fabric under the master pattern (page 103). Position the appliqués in place on the background fabric in numbered order.

5. Following the manufacturer's instructions, fuse the appliqué shapes to the background fabric.

6. Stitch the appliqué shapes to the background fabric using the desired decorative stitch.

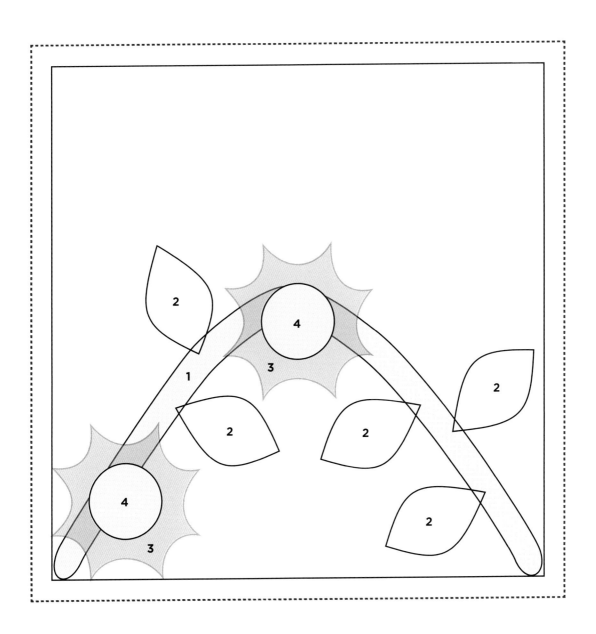

16 | Combed Swag

Skill Level: Beginner

1. Trace the appliqué patterns onto a lightweight fusible web, such as Steam-A-Seam 2. Roughly cut out each shape from the fusible web, but do not cut on the marked line.

2. Following the manufacturer's instructions, fuse the adhesive to the wrong side of the appliqué fabrics. Use a sharp scissors to cut out the appliqué shapes on the marked lines. Take care when cutting to avoid fraying the edges of the fabric.

3. Remove the paper from the back of the cut appliqué shapes, leaving a fine layer of adhesive on the back of fabric.

4. Cut a 6½" (16.5 cm) piece of background fabric. Position the background fabric under the master pattern (page 103). Position the appliqués in place on the background fabric.

5. Following the manufacturer's instructions, fuse the appliqué shapes to the background fabric.

6. 6. Stitch the appliqué shapes to the background fabric using the desired decorative stitch.

17 | Orange Peel

Skill Level: Beginner

Appliqué Instructions for a 6-Inch Finished Block

1. Trace four A units onto sew-in interfacing (Be sure to use interfacing for use with sheer to light fabrics). Trace the shape in the finished size, without a seam allowance. Leave enough space between each traced shape for a very generous seam allowance.

2. Layer the interfacing on top of the appliqué fabric, with the right side of the fabric up. Pin the interfacing and appliqué fabric together to prevent shifting.

3. Stitch on the marked line, all the way around the shape, leaving no gaps. Use either a regular straight stitch and the feed dogs up, or free motion stitching with the feed dogs down. If you are comfortable with free motion sewing, this is an easier way to handle tight corners and small details.

4. Trim around the appliqué shape with a scant ¼" to ⅛" (6 mm to 3 mm) seam allowance. Clip the seam allowance at corners and curves.

5. Clip a slit in the interfacing. Take care not to cut into the appliqué fabric.

6. Turn the appliqué shape right-side out through the slit in the interfacing.

7. Use a bone folder or chopstick to smooth out the seams and corners. Press with a warm iron since most interfacings are made of polyester, and too hot of an iron may melt polyester interfacing.

8. Stitch the appliqué shape to the background fabric using a blind hemstitch and invisible monofilament thread.

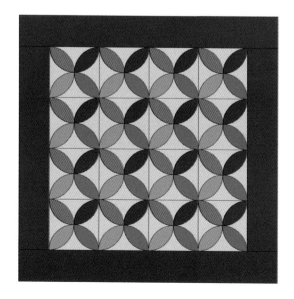

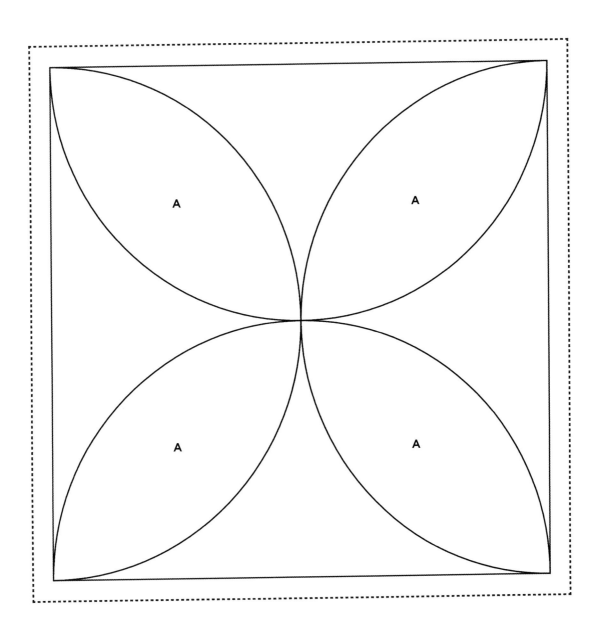

18 | Spring Beauty

Skill Level: Intermediate

1. Stitch the A triangle units to each side of the B square unit, pressing the seams toward A.

2. Stitch the two C strips of fabric together. Press the seam allowance open.

3. Trace the pattern for the C unit on the back side of the fabric strip, matching the seam line on the pattern piece with the seam line on the strip set. Make 4.

4. Finish the remainder of the block following the instructions for the Orange Peel block (page 136).

What gives this block added interest is the ability to color the pieces so it appears as if the orange peel is transparent across the on-point square.

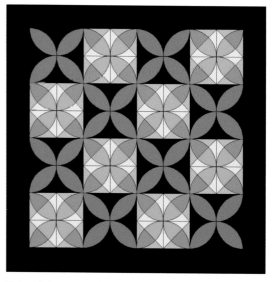

This quilt layout combines two blocks: Orange Peel (page 136) and Spring Beauty.

Cutting Instructions for One Block

Unit	Sub-cut	Quantity	6" (15.24 cm) Finished	9" (23 cm) Finished	12" (30 cm) Finished
A	 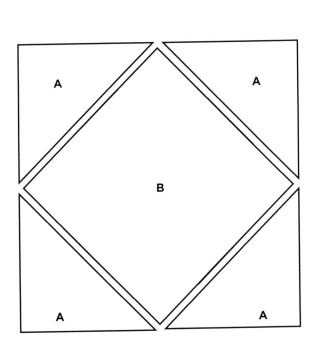	2	3⅞" × 3⅞" (9.75 × 9.75 cm)	5⅜" × 5⅜" (13.75 × 13.75 cm)	6⅞" × 6⅞" (17.5 × 17.5 cm)
B		1	4¾" × 4¾" (12 × 12 cm)	6⅞" × 6⅞" (17.5 × 17.5 cm)	9" × 9" (23 × 23 cm)
C		1—Color 1 1—Color 2	2¼" × 16" (5.75 × 40.75 cm)	3" × 22" (7.6 × 56 cm)	3⅝" × 27" (9 × 68.5 cm)

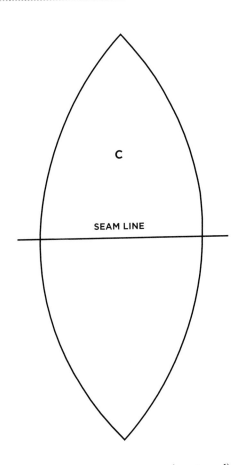

C

SEAM LINE

(continued)

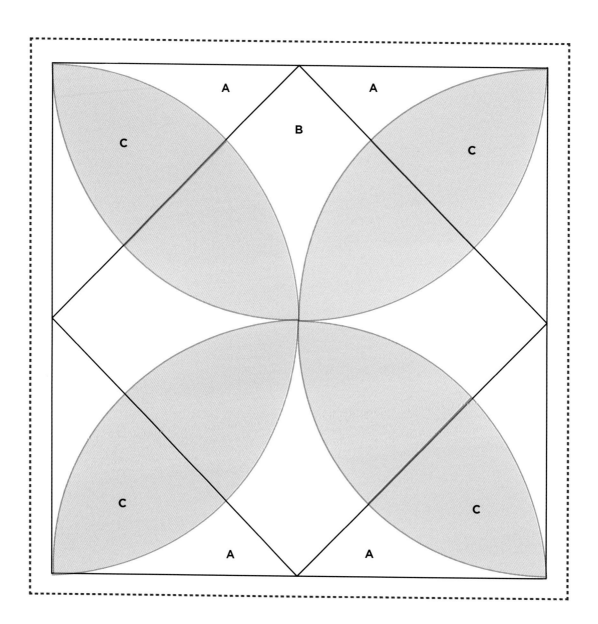

About the Author

Nancy Wick is a textile artist and longarm quilter with a passion for teaching others about how to get the most joy from their sewing machines. Nancy made her first quilt in the early 1990s— a queen-sized traditional sampler quilt—and has never looked back. She enjoys combining traditional blocks with a modern, contemporary twist by paying attention to color, surface embellishment, thread work, and technology. Her work often includes hand-dyed or hand-painted fabric. As a former IT professional, Nancy enjoys finding ways to incorporate her fancy, computerized sewing machines in innovative ways into her craft.

Nancy lives in St. Paul, Minnesota, with her husband and three Bengal cats, who are known affectionately as her "kids with fur."

Photo by Nancy Jordan

Quilting Resources

The Original Little Foot ¼" Presser Foot
www.littlefoot.net

Hoffman Fabrics www.hoffmanfabrics.com

Art Gallery Fabrics www.artgalleryfabrics.com

Kai Scissors Some great choices for appliqué
www.kaiscissors.com

Superior Threads www.superiorthreads.com

Electric Quilt www.electricquilt.com

Index